Who Is My God?

An Innovative Guide to Finding Your Spiritual Identity

2nd Edition

Created by the Editors at SkyLight Paths

Walking Together, Finding the Way
SKYLIGHT PATHS Publishing
Woodstock, Vermont

Who Is My God? 2nd Edition
An Innovative Guide to Finding Your Spiritual Identity

First Printing 2004
© 2004 and 2000 by SkyLight Paths Publishing

Library of Congress Cataloging-in-Publication Data
Who is my God? : an innovative guide to finding your spiritual identity / created by the editors at SkyLight Paths.—2nd ed.
p. cm.
Includes bibliographical references and index.
ISBN 1-59473-014-8 (pbk.)
1. Spiritual life. 2. Self-evaluation. 3. Religions. I. SkyLight Paths Publishing.
BL624.W512 2004
204—dc22

2004001566

10 9 8 7 6 5 4 3 2 1

Manufactured in the United States of America

SkyLight Paths Publishing is creating a place where people of different spiritual traditions come together for challenge and inspiration, a place where we can help each other understand the mystery that lies at the heart of our existence.

SkyLight Paths sees both believers and seekers as a community that increasingly transcends traditional boundaries of religion and denomination—people wanting to learn from each other, *walking together, finding the way.*

SkyLight Paths, "Walking Together, Finding the Way" and colophon are trademarks of LongHill Partners, Inc., registered in the U.S. Patent and Trademark Office.

Walking Together, Finding the Way
Published by SkyLight Paths Publishing
A Division of LongHill Partners, Inc.
Sunset Farm Offices, Route 4, P.O. Box 237
Woodstock, VT 05091
Tel: (802) 457-4000   Fax: (802) 457-4004
www.skylightpaths.com

Contents

PART ONE

Finding Your Spiritual Identity

1 ›
What Is a Spiritual Identity?

If you have picked up this book, odds are good that you are seeking answers to spiritual questions. Or, perhaps you know someone who is. We, too, are seeking. We who have created this guide—the editors at SkyLight Paths Publishing—have designed it out of our own lives. *Who Is My God?* doesn't answer all of our questions about spirituality, and it will not eliminate all of yours either—it is not intended to. But what it will do is help you see your unique spiritual path more clearly, or if you're just beginning to consider the spiritual, to find a path that's suited to who you are on the deepest level.

Gandhi said that there are as many spiritualities in the world as there are people. We couldn't agree with this statement more. On many levels, all of us are probably seeking the same things in life—but we pursue them by different paths. His Holiness the Dalai Lama, one of the most influential spiritual leaders of our time, recently said: "For my part, meeting innumerable others from all over the world and from every walk of life reminds me of our basic sameness as human beings. Indeed, the more I see of the world, the clearer it becomes that no matter what our situation, whether we are rich or poor, educated or not, of one race, gender, religion or another, we all desire to be happy and to avoid suffering. Our every intended action, in a sense our whole life—how we choose to live it within the context of the limitations imposed by our circumstances—can be seen as our answer to the great question which confronts us all: 'How am I to be happy?'"[1] He is right—we are similar in what we desire but not in how we find it.

Your spiritual path is how you answer basic questions like "How am I to be happy?" It is uniquely your own and does not fit a fixed pattern. Just as we all learn differently, we approach the spiritual differently.

Sometimes we even feel the conflict of different paths to spiritual understanding *within* ourselves. As was said of the great seventeenth-century Japanese poet and spiritual seeker Basho, whose personal journeys were as much metaphorical as they were literal: "As we turn every corner of the Narrow Road to the Deep North, we sometimes stand up unawares to applaud and we sometimes fall flat to resist the agonizing pains we feel in the depths of our hearts. There are also times when we feel like taking to the road ourselves, seizing the raincoat lying near by, or times when we feel like sitting down till our legs take root, enjoying the scene we picture before our eyes."[2]

Each of our spiritual searches is unique and special, regardless of whether or not we live our lives within religious or spiritual traditions. Faith traditions provide us with scriptures, spiritual practices, rituals, and communities, but they cannot control how we actually relate to those elements and use them. (If anyone tells you differently, they may not be talking about a religion, but about something that might better be called a cult.)

Your Spiritual Identity is already within you. Centuries ago, the Spanish nun Teresa of Ávila wrote a simple book called *The Interior Castle,* about building a relationship with the Divine. In it she said: "It seems I'm saying something foolish. For if this castle is the soul, clearly one doesn't have to enter it since it is within oneself. How foolish it would seem were we to tell someone to enter a room he is already in. But you must understand that there is a great difference in the ways one may be inside the castle."

How different people should use this book differently

Who Is My God? is for three types of people. First, it is for those of us who live out our spiritual lives within a religious tradition; who, either consciously or unconsciously, sometimes need help defining or clarifying what we believe as we struggle between faith and doubt—an exercise common for many people.

Second, this book is for those of us who pursue spiritual practice *outside* religious traditions, who have experience exploring new avenues of spiritual understanding. We sometimes need help finding learning resources or a community for spiritual growth. For us, the question is not so much "*Is* there a spiritual path that is uniquely my own?"—yes, of course there is! The questions of importance for us are, rather, "Where are the other people who think like me?" and "What are some other resources that will help me to grow?" This book should help in figuring that out.

Third, this book is for those of us who have never become involved in religion or spiritual practice, or those of us who have deliberately opted out of both. We have a Spiritual Identity that may be unexplored—a latent and tantalizing possibility. If you are in this category, the discovery of your Spiritual Identity can be a life-changing event.

So, what *is* a Spiritual Identity?

A Spiritual Identity is the pattern of beliefs, attitudes, and feelings about the Sacred and the world—a pattern that defines who you are at the profoundest level. Discovering your Spiritual Identity is akin to uncovering the meaning of your life.

We find that many people when seriously exploring their Spiritual Identity for the first time have many "Aha!" experiences that go along with the discovery. Leo Tolstoy's realization was dramatic indeed: "A voice seemed to cry within me.…'To know God and to live are one. God is life.' Live to seek God, and life will not be without God. And stronger than ever rose up life within and around me, and the light that then shone never left me again. Thus I was saved from self-murder. When and how this change in me took place I could not say."[3]

If you are seeking to understand your Spiritual Identity for the first time, you may suddenly understand the underlying reasons for certain decisions you have made or paths you have taken. It can be like discovering your subconscious for the first time, with the same "I didn't know I had one!" kind of realization. The world suddenly looks different.

Sometimes these realizations are less sudden, as your Spiritual Identity grows with you over a period of time. The author Kathleen Norris, who realized her own true identity in midlife by coming to terms with her conservative Christian upbringing, explains her path this way: "Fear is not a bad place to start a spiritual journey. If you know what makes you afraid, you can see more clearly that the way out is through the fear. For me, this has meant acknowledging that the strong emotions dredged up by the Christian worship services—usually weddings or funerals—I attended during the twenty-year period when I would have described my religion as 'nothing' were trying to tell me something. It has meant coming to terms with my fundamentalist Methodist ancestors, no longer ignoring them but respecting their power."[4]

No spiritual path is supposed to be easy, and discovering yours is only a starting point for becoming who you are destined to become. Don't be discouraged if your life does not change overnight—it probably won't! Here we will not only show you how to discover your

Spiritual Identity for yourself, but give you resources to get started integrating and deepening it in your life.

Are we *born* with a Spiritual Identity?

You may have been born into a faith tradition or you may have grown up worshiping within one because a loved one taught you how, but your personal Spiritual Identity is about more than that. You are not born with your Spiritual Identity already intact. It comprises *how* you believe (your Spiritual Type™) and *what* you believe (your Tradition Indicator).

Involvement in a religious or spiritual tradition surely influences your Spiritual Identity, but in ways that you don't even realize. Your Spiritual Identity is created by many other factors as well: experiences you have, dreams you dream, people you meet, ideas you ponder. One of the purposes of this book is to help show you your Spiritual Identity so that you can begin to explore it deliberately. We all develop our Spiritual Identities in ways that can be different for each one of us: spiritual reading, meditation, prayer, worship, retreats, the celebration of life cycle events, ritual, and spiritual exercise, just to name a few.

As you unravel your Spiritual Identity, it is important to remember this principle: most people need the help or perspective of others in order to grow. Buddhist monk and teacher Thich Nhat Hanh says it this way:

> Let us visualize the ocean with a multitude of waves. Imagine that we are a wave on the ocean, and surrounding us are many, many waves. If the wave looks deeply within herself, she will realize that her being there depends on the presence of all the other waves. Her coming up, her going down, and her being big or small depend entirely on how the other waves are. Looking into yourself, you touch the whole, you touch everything—you are conditioned by what is there around you.[5]

Our Spiritual Identity is not only *what* we believe but *how* we believe, and we cannot always be aware of our own beliefs, feelings, and behavior. Sometimes they are below the surface of our consciousness. That is why most spiritual experts agree that it is not wise to live your spiritual life in a vacuum. We need the perspective of others—help along the way—in order to grow.

In his book *Honey from the Rock*, Lawrence Kushner makes an analogy about how each one of us carries around an incomplete jigsaw puzzle. As we move through life, we meet various people, each of whom holds one of the pieces to our puzzle—and we often do not know they have it until they give it to us.[6] That is often how discovering a Spiritual Identity works, either suddenly or more gradually, over time. All of our puzzles are incomplete in some way. Hopefully, this book will help you with one or two of the pieces that may be missing from yours.

2›

What Does My Spiritual Identity Have to Do with Religion?

"I am spiritual, *not* religious," people often say. And, it's true. More people in America pray, meditate, do yoga and other spiritual practices—and believe in a higher power—than ever before. Ninety to ninety-five percent of Americans typically respond that they believe in God. Despite this, attendance at services of most faiths has declined steadily since the early 1960s. Why?

> "Religion has hurt many people."
> "Religion leaves no room for self-expression."
> "Religion is boring."
> "Religion only tells us what we are *supposed* to believe."

The list could go on. These accusations often have truth in them, and as a result most Americans remain *spiritual*, even when they are not—or are no longer—religious.

"Should You Design Your Own Religion?" asked a recent *Utne Reader* headline. No, answer most spiritual teachers; choose a primary path and follow it. The Buddhist meditation teacher Sylvia

Boorstein writes: "The pitfall of inventing your own practice…is that you have no way of judging spiritual progress if you're completely alone. There's no substantial group of other people to keep tabs on you."[1]

Similarly, the Catholic priest and monk Father Thomas Keating says: "When you make a collage of various traditions, you run the risk of digging too many wells in a desert, which might take a lot of time, whereas if you work one well that has a good reputation, where water is to be found, it might be more rewarding in the long term. Information about other traditions can complement and enrich your particular path, but you need to be well rooted before you can derive any true benefit."[2]

This is all well and good, but many of us need help just getting started. How do we begin discovering—or sometimes simply clarifying—our Spiritual Identity? Reading these chapters, taking the Spiritual Identity Self-Test™, tabulating your results, and carefully reviewing the various brief descriptions of faiths and spiritual traditions will help you to begin.

We live in a time of *new spirituality*

In the not-too-distant past, *spirituality* simply meant *religion* for most of us, and religion was simply what we were born with. For most of us today, the spiritual environment is very different.

We are exposed to so many options. More than ever, our lives intersect with those of people of other faiths. Even if most of us raise our children with less specific religious training than our parents gave us, we are often more attuned to their spiritual growth than our parents were to ours. Today, spiritual growth does not necessarily equal religious involvement. Spiritual insight is looked for, and found, in many new places.

The new spirituality also has important implications for people involved in religious traditions. Again, in the recent past, Catholics and Jews, Buddhists and Baptists, Wiccans and Hindus rarely met or talked with each other. Today, we are more often in daily contact with each other; we live or work side-by-side—we even marry each other and are faced with the question of how to raise children together. We sometimes make the mistake of thinking that participation in a religious tradition prevents us from participating in—or learning from—other spiritualities. But it is one of the great features of spiritual life in America that we now regularly interact with people of other spiritual and religious traditions. In fact, for many, such interaction is now an important means of spiritual growth. Our spiritual lives are richer because of it.

Today's new spirituality is found in an increasingly common feeling of openness to learning from faiths other than our own, and in an atmosphere where this is possible without feeling threatened. You can indeed learn from people of other faiths without leaving your own.

Also, more and more, religious traditions allow us the flexibility to evolve our spiritual understandings over time. We need not accept one set of truths now and forever; we can often remain within a religious tradition as we change our minds. Professor and author Marcus J. Borg describes his experience within Christianity this way: "My childhood notion of God, with refinements, persisted for about three decades. In childhood, I believed in this notion of God without difficulty; in my early teens, I began to have doubts about it; in my twenties, the doubts became disbelief; but through this whole process, the same notion of God persisted. It was what I believed and then disbelieved. Compared to that notion of God, the God I have come to know since is the God I never knew."[3] Most religious traditions acknowledge today that belief evolves over time.

The difference between spirituality and religion

The real difference between spirituality and religion might be expressed like this: spirituality is your own, and religion is something you share with others. Abu Hamid Muhammad Ghazali, a Muslim mystic who lived a millennium ago, describes the difference between spirituality and religion in his life, this way:

> I thus comprehended their fundamental teachings on the intellectual side, and progressed, as far as is possible by study and oral instruction, in the knowledge of mysticism. It became clear to me, however, that what is most distinctive of mysticism is something which cannot be apprehended by study, but only by immediate experience....What a difference there is between *knowing* the definition of health and satiety, together with their causes and presuppositions, and *being* healthy and satisfied![4]

Every religion is full of spiritualities, and spirituality can be cultivated both within a particular religious tradition as well as outside of it. There are Christian spiritualities, Jewish spiritualities, Hindu spiritualities, Buddhist spiritualities, Muslim spiritualities, New Consciousness spiritualities, Humanist spiritualities, and so on. This book will explain them to you, and knowing your Spiritual Identity will help you identify the one that matches you the best.

If you describe yourself as "spiritual"—and many of us do—you may already be engaged in spiritual practices of various kinds: prayer, meditation, and yoga are common ones. What you may not realize is that most spiritual practices have their origins in religious traditions. For instance, in addition to the spiritual practices listed above, the following practices often considered today as new all have their roots in religion: mindfulness, kabbalah, *feng-shui*, *qigong*, and centering prayer. When something is referred to as "an ancient spiritual practice," its origins can most often be traced to religion in one way or another. Religious traditions are rich with resources for the spiritual life.

Sometimes we need to look at religion in a new light

One of the best ways to deepen our spiritual lives is to explore the wealth of religious traditions. Chapters 5–7 will help you to do that, providing entrances to twenty-eight spiritualities—descriptions of faiths, denominations, and spiritual paths that can serve as starting points for you to explore your Spiritual Identity further. Many of these may be familiar to you—some in name only—while others represent more recent movements, rediscovered traditions, and less commonly known spiritualities. Maybe you can find a home among them. Or maybe you will simply learn from these other faiths in a way that enhances your own. At the least you can discover fascinating thinkers, ideas, rituals, and celebrations that speak to the seeker in all of us. If you have been unsure about religion in the past—as opposed to spirituality—you may need to try seeing religion in a new light.

None of us has a Spiritual Identity that relates to only one spiritual tradition

When you uncover the spiritual tradition that best matches what you believe, you will also find other spiritual traditions that you can learn from. These are often equally important. As mentioned earlier, when we identify with a particular spiritual tradition, we can still benefit from interacting with, and learning from, others. Before you finish this book you will be introduced to many such opportunities.

We often choose a spiritual tradition or place of worship because it is where we feel most comfortable—and we often *should* choose this way—but just as visiting another country can enlarge our perspective on our homeland, visiting another tradition can stimulate spiritual growth in revelatory ways.

For example, if you come from a tradition rich in ritual, encountering one that is more simple and austere can open up untapped, subtle ways of perceiving beauty. This might, for instance, represent the difference between Tibetan Buddhism and Zen, among Buddhist spiritualities, or the difference between Roman Catholicism and Quakerism, among Christian spiritualities. Likewise, if your religious background encourages logical and rational thinking in matters of faith, encountering contemplative, mystical traditions can transform your way of thinking. You will discover more about these differences when you uncover your Spiritual Type, the first component of your Spiritual Identity.

There is a story common to several faith traditions in which a person leaves home in search of truth, travelling to a faraway place. In that place lives a very wise person who is known for providing answers. When she arrives in the faraway place and asks her question, the traveler learns from the wise one that the truth she sought was at home all the time. Yet the journey's usefulness is never questioned: the purpose of the journey is to show the truth that we cannot always see when we are at home.

3 ›
What Is the Spiritual Identity Self-Test™?

The Spiritual Identity Self-Test is designed to help you uncover your Spiritual Identity by recording your responses to eighty-seven statements, each answered multiple choice. Each answer is important and combines with the others to create a profile of your basic spiritual beliefs, feelings, and behavior.

The eighty-seven statements are divided into two parts: Part One comprises the first twenty-four statements, and your answers to these will uncover your Spiritual Type. Part Two is composed of the remaining sixty-three statements, and your answers to these will uncover the second component of your Spiritual Identity—your Tradition Indicator.

The test was developed by the editorial team at SkyLight Paths Publishing, a diverse group of people representing a variety of spiritual traditions, and was then "field-tested" by dozens of others—people of all faiths and backgrounds—to fine-tune the various result possibilities. Each person answered a series of questions about taking the test and their results. We then asked spiritual and religious experts representing Hinduism, Judaism, Islam, New Consciousness,

Protestantism, Catholicism, Sufism, Buddhism, and several other traditions to take the test and offer feedback based on their experiences and results. With this valuable input, each of the statements in the test—particularly the sixty-three in Part Two—reached their final form.

Who should take the test?

The Spiritual Identity Self-Test is designed for use by individuals, but it is also ideal for some groups. Book discussion groups with a penchant for spiritual conversations, for instance, will enjoy taking the test together and discussing the results. Religious groups can use Part One of the test, in particular, to understand differences and resolve conflicts. Couples can take the test in order to better understand each other: Your mate's opinions on these issues may show up later in a wide range of important occasions, including discussions about how to raise a child, when it is right to end a life, and how to spend money. Families will also enjoy taking the test together. Often family members assume that they know each other's Spiritual Identity, when in reality they don't. The test results often spark conversations that can lead to greater understanding within the family.

The test is also ideal for use by chaplains, clergy, counselors, and spiritual directors as a resource for gaining insight into the people from diverse faiths and backgrounds that they now so frequently encounter in their pastoral work. (See p. 144 to learn about how to become a Spiritual Identity Self-Test facilitator for both individuals and groups.)

Many people who use *Who Is My God?* and who take the Spiritual Identity Self-Test go through this process by themselves—and this can be the best way for some of us. When we are alone, we are the most honest about what we think, how we behave, and how we feel.

Also, for those of us who may be naturally averse to talking about personal issues like spirituality, the self-test is especially useful for creating in a book an experience of community.

The test is designed to be accurate and useful for people already involved in religion or interested in spirituality, as well as for people with no previous involvement at all. If you are new to thinking about spiritual matters, the test is a good first step. On the other hand, we find that many people who have spent years in one spiritual practice and then another, or who have moved from one religious tradition to another, find new meaning for their spiritual lives by taking the test.

As with all such tests, some of the statements may be difficult for you to answer simply. You will likely have immediate responses to many of the statements; you can expect that others will seem ambiguous and confusing. In each case, select your best answer for each: a, b, c, or d. The test is designed to accommodate occasional ambiguity.

Spiritual Types™: *How* we believe

The test will first help you discover your Spiritual Type. Your Spiritual Type is the result of your responses to the first twenty-four statements, and a measure of *how* you believe what you believe.

There are four Spiritual Types:

> *Faithful-Rational*
> *Faithful-Contemplative*
> *Skeptical-Rational*
> *Skeptical-Contemplative*

Brief descriptions of each Spiritual Type are found at the end of Chapter 4, pages 31–33.

How is a Spiritual Type™ similar to a personality type?

Most of us are familiar with personality type tests, such as the Myers-Briggs Type Indicator. You may even know your personality type according to one of these systems, and you may have used testing procedures like this to help you determine a career path or your compatibility with a possible mate. Your Spiritual Type is similar—and different.

Most personality type tests aim to measure what C. G. Jung called the dynamic interaction of the patterns of human behavior common in each of us. For instance, Jung believed that when our minds are engaged and active, we are either *judging* (organizing, evaluating) or *perceiving* (observing). We are born with a predisposition to one or the other, and we develop that tendency throughout our lives in various ways. We use our dominant function to make both basic and complex decisions; understanding that we have this kind of tendency helps us see how our lives are constructed.

A Spiritual Type works in related ways. The features of our spiritual makeup interact in dynamic ways as we, for instance, tend toward either active or passive spiritual practices, and between Rational, Skeptical, Contemplative, or Faithful spiritual behavior. The dynamic interaction of our spiritual beliefs, feelings, and behavior are at the root of how our lives are constructed and how we see the world.

Whereas a *personality* type may tell you whether or not you tend to make decisions based on past experience or by following hunches, a *Spiritual* Type may tell you something like whether or not you tend to believe there are many paths to truth or only one right path. Your Spiritual Type helps you understand past behavior and decisions; it helps you know why and where you may have disagreed with a friend or loved one on spiritual matters. Like your personality type, your Spiritual Type takes into account not just your ideas but your feelings and behavior, too.

Spiritual Types point to how we show our spirituality in ways that are sometimes subtle. Someone could discover your Spiritual Type by talking with the people closest to you, by asking what you talk about, how you spend your money, how you spend your free time. Even if you never talk about spirituality, your life shows what you believe about many important things in the ways you act and respond to what is around you.

What else can my Spiritual Type™ tell me?

Your Spiritual Type will help you understand how your core Spiritual Identity may be similar to or different from that of the people you love most. Realizing that a partner or loved one sees things spiritual in a way radically different from your own can be a revelatory experience. Thus potential mates can benefit greatly from understanding each other's Spiritual Type. If you worship within a religious tradition or community, your Spiritual Type can help you to understand your personal contribution to the group. People within groups can come to better understand each other—and sometimes resolve conflict—by discussing the differences and similarities between Spiritual Types.

Your Spiritual Type also helps you understand some of the subtle ways you exhibit your beliefs and practice without even knowing it. Most of us do not talk "spiritual talk" all the time, easily telling others about who we are spiritually. Our lives are subtler than that. After you tabulate your results to the self-test you will read a brief description of your Spiritual Type; this will give you some basic language to use in talking about your Spiritual Identity, if you choose to. It will also be helpful to read each of the other brief Spiritual Type descriptions in order to find the ones that might best match your experience of friends or loved ones.

What if I disagree with my results?

Although based on sound scientific principles, a personality test cannot offer conclusive, irrefutable results. Neither can a spirituality test. In fact, spirituality tests cannot claim to be based on such scientific principles. There simply is no scientific data that helps us understand the human spirit—and there probably never will be. Discovering your Spiritual Type is not a science. Your spirit and soul are too complex, too inexplicable for that.

Don't assume that your results are set in stone. If you disagree with yours, take Part One again, and if you still disagree, discuss the issues with a friend. (You also may want to use p. 144 to contact us.) Remember, more important than the actual "test results" you get are the *ideas* the text itself causes you to think about, regarding who you are spiritually; these ideas can provide the impetus to help you delve deeper into your beliefs and to understand what they mean to who you are.

Spiritual & religious traditions: *what* we believe

Part Two of the test helps you uncover the second component of your Spiritual Identity: your Tradition Indicator—the spiritual tradition that best matches *what* you believe. It not only gauges *what* you believe but what you don't believe. It shows what questions you are most interested in asking. Psychologist Sam Keen recently said: "What shapes our lives are the questions we ask, refuse to ask, or never think of asking....What you ask is who you are. What you find depends on what you search for."[1]

When you tabulate your results, you will see with which of the major religious or spiritual traditions your Spiritual Identity fits most closely. There are twenty-eight traditions described; you will have the opportunity to read about them all in Chapters 5–7. Again, do not be concerned if some statements are difficult for you to respond to—this is to be expected. Occasional uncertain responses will not skew your results. The tabulation is based on your responses to the statements with which you can positively agree. These are the questions you are asking—the answers you are finding.

You *create* your Spiritual Identity

Personality typing is mostly concerned with understanding what you were born with. In contrast, you were born with an undeveloped personal Spiritual Identity—your spiritual beliefs, feelings, and practices hadn't even begun yet. (You may have been born a Christian, a Jew, or a Hindu but, as discussed above, that's altogether different.) You *create* your personal spiritual path, and understanding where you stand today will help you become the spiritual person you want to become tomorrow.

4›

Take the Test

Part One

The response sheet for taking Part One of the Spiritual Identity Self-Test is located on page 24. You may photocopy this page if more than one person is taking the test. While taking the test, respond to every statement—don't skip any or it will skew your results; however, the test is designed so that you can answer occasional questions more tentatively and it will still tabulate accurately. Take the test by yourself or with others. Read each statement and mark your response by placing a checkmark in the appropriate letter column on the response sheet. Use the following letters for each response:

a = I agree completely
b = I agree somewhat
c = I don't agree
d = Not applicable to me/I don't think that way

First, take Part One, responding to each of the twenty-four statements. Mark your answers to this first set of statements on the response sheet. You will not tabulate your Part One responses until you also complete Part Two.

Answer Sheet: Part One—Your Spiritual Type™

Section F					Section S					Section R					Section C				
	a	b	c	d		a	b	c	d		a	b	c	d		a	b	c	d
1					2					3					4				
5					6					7					8				
9					10					11					12				
13					14					15					16				
17					18					19					20				
21					22					23					24				
TOTALS:																			
A+B=																			

Use the following letters for each response:

a = I agree completely
b = I agree somewhat
c = I don't agree
d = Not applicable to me/I don't think that way

The Spiritual Identity Self-Test™: Part One

1. There is one way to truth.
2. There is no way to know for sure whether God exists.
3. The joyous spiritual feelings people experience are often unrelated to real spiritual understanding.
4. Intimacy with the Divine comes primarily through direct encounter, meditation, prayer, and other personal paths of spiritual experience.
5. Faith is the starting point for any spiritual life.
6. Ultimately we each face the mysteries of life alone.

7. Faith is well-grounded belief.

8. Spiritual truth is discovered more within oneself than in books.

9. The way to eliminate doubt is through faith.

10. It is not necessary to have religious faith in order to be spiritual.

11. Spirituality begins with having a basic set of beliefs.

12. In the search for what is true, the heart is the ultimate guide.

13. Spiritual understanding has a divine source.

14. Religions are relics of the past—and in most ways irrelevant for us today.

15. Belief should be the result of reliable evidence.

16. Living a spiritual life means increasing our ability to see the Divine all around us.

17. Holy scriptures are our most reliable resource for knowing how to live.

18. Religious commitment is unnecessary for living a spiritual life.

19. The ability to express *what* you believe is one of the most important tests of faith.

20. Nothing about the Ultimate Reality can adequately be expressed by words.

21. The gift of faith can be sudden, complete, and everlasting.

22. There are some things that we are not supposed to understand—and the Divine is one of them.

23. Increasing one's knowledge is the most reliable way to truth.

24. We should not strive to explain the Divine; we should rather strive to experience the Divine directly.

Part Two

Now that you have completed Part One of the test, move on to Part Two. The response sheet for Part Two can be found on page 26. Part Two consists of sixty-three statements, which you answer using the same response options used in Part One.

Answer Sheet: Part Two—Your Tradition Indicator

Section C				Section B				Section J				Section I				Section H				Section N				Section U			
a	b	c	d	a	b	c	d	a	b	c	d	a	b	c	d	a	b	c	d	a	b	c	d	a	b	c	d
1				2				3				4				5				6				7				
8				9				10				11				12				13				14				
15				16				17				18				19				20				21				
22				23				24				25				26				27				28				
29				30				31				32				33				34				35				
36				37				38				39				40				41				42				
43				44				45				46				47				48				49				
50				51				52				53				54				55				56				
57				58				59				60				61				62				63				
TOTALS: **A+B =**																											

Use the following letters for each response:

a = I agree completely; **b** = I agree somewhat; **c** = I don't agree; **d** = Not applicable to me/I don't think that way

The Spiritual Identity Self-Test™: Part Two

1. God has come to earth in human form.

2. Our perception of an individual "self" is an illusion.

3. God's name is ultimately unspeakable, unknowable.

4. Believers are all called by God to become a single community of faith.

5. God contains many opposites. God is both Creator and Destroyer.

6. Religion usually hinders spirituality.

7. We are accountable only to ourselves and to each other for our actions.

8. Acknowledgment of and repentance for sin is the first step in a relationship with God.

9. We are capable of comprehending the truth entirely through our own efforts.

10. God is the author and guide of everything that has been created.

11. God has been revealed to the world primarily through a series of prophets, including Jesus and Muhammad.

12. Each of us is part of God, in the way a tiny drop of water is a part of the ocean.

13. The recovery of the Divine Feminine is an urgent need of our age.

14. Choosing not to believe in an unproven afterlife liberates us to live fully in the present.

15. To love God and your neighbor sums up the essence of God's law.

16. Knowing whether or not God exists has no particular bearing on living a spiritual life.

17. The Divine has no form whatsoever.

18. God is both merciful and just, in perfectly equal balance.

19. The Divine is capable of appearing in innumerable manifestations, and has done so throughout time, throughout the world.

20. Relying upon the wisdom of our higher self is the one sure spiritual path.

21. It is impossible to know what happens after we die. The only honest view is that our consciousness expires along with our bodies.

22. The original sin of humanity destroyed some of our original intimacy with God—intimacy that will be restored and surpassed in Heaven.

23. The most common characteristic of human life is suffering; the most worthy spiritual goal is the elimination of suffering—our own, as well as that of others.

24. There is an era of peace and justice coming that will arrive through the cooperation of all people with God's help.

25. In each age, the prophets of God are sent to establish God's justice on earth.

26. Each of us goes through a cycle of death and rebirth with the purpose of gaining wisdom and of ultimately becoming one with God.

27. We are all divine by nature.

28. There is nothing from which we need to be saved.

29. The Bible is the inspired word of God.

30. The idea that we each have an individual soul is an illusion.

31. Moses was the first and most important prophet.

32. Submitting to the will of God is more important than asking God to grant our requests.

33. The Divine can be worshiped in many forms.

34. Every person is his or her own best judge of their own personal way to God.

35. The idea of God is simply an externalization of unrealized qualities and aspirations found in all of us.

36. God is a Trinity of Persons—a mystery of unity in diversity.

37. Nothing we perceive to exist—including our soul—lasts forever.

38. Keeping God's commandments is the primary way of living a spiritual life.

39. It is possible for war to be justifiable, but only when it is a holy struggle against evil.

40. The eternal and uncreated universe we inhabit undergoes cycles of creation and destruction.

41. We live in an era of new consciousness, in which we can experience entirely new levels of spiritual understanding.

42. It is our duty to liberate all people from oppression—institutional, religious, or otherwise.

43. The incarnation of God into the world is a unique and unrepeatable event.

44. Spiritual practices are a means to enlightenment.

45. God is present in all things.

46. Everything belongs to God; we are merely caretakers of our possessions, and we should be generous with them.

47. Image-worship is an important step on the way to God.

48. Only by reclaiming and honoring the Earth as sacred will the world find balance and harmony.

49. Traditional religions are nothing but relics of the past.

50. Salvation comes through faith, by God's grace.

51. Each of us has our own *karma* to deal with—the accumulation of our past deeds both good and bad.

52. We are called by God to repair the world.

53. We find salvation through devotion to God in this life, and through obedience to God's commands.

54. Truth is One; the wise have given it many names.

55. The imagination and the self are divine.

56. Critical intelligence liberates us from the need to rely on faith.

57. Faith without good deeds is dead.

58. Wisdom and compassion are the supreme spiritual values.

59. Created in God's image, we each have free will and a powerful moral capacity.

60. The spiritual life is incomplete without charity—the sharing of one's material wealth with others.

61. Death is only a shedding of the body—after which the soul moves on to a new incarnation.

62. Spiritual growth comes more through spiritual practices than traditional religious observance.

63. After death we live on, but only in the memories of the living.

Tabulate your results for Part One: Discover your Spiritual Type™

The next step in this process of spiritual discovery is to tabulate the results of your answers to Part One and Part Two of the Spiritual Identity Self-Test—eighty-seven statements in all.

Step 1

Your responses to the twenty-four statements of Part One are organized into four vertical sections, marked F, S, R, and C. Look at the first section—labeled Section F. Your responses within Section F are organized into four vertical columns: a, b, c, and d. Tabulate the total number of *a*'s and *b*'s and enter that total in the box provided, as in the sample at right.

Now, do the same for each of the other three sections in Part One. Write those numbers in the appropriate boxes on your response sheet.

Section F			
	a	b	c	d
1	✓			
5				✓
9			✓	
13	✓			
17		✓		
21				✓
TOTALS:	2	1		
A+B=	3			

Step 2

Next, look at the totals you have written in each of the four boxes. Two of these totals determine the first important element of your

Spiritual Type. Look first at Section F and Section S—which of these two boxes has the highest total?

Write that letter here: (F or S) _____

Look now at Section R and Section C—which box has the highest total? (This is the second element of your Spiritual Type.)

Write that letter here: (R or C) _____

These two letters form your Spiritual Type. They are a key to *how* you believe what you believe, and how and where you seek spiritual growth. For instance, is the spiritual side of life important to you? Do you talk much about it? Do you believe more with your head or your heart? Or, do you have more doubt and skepticism than belief? Do you learn more from experience than from scriptures or texts? Do you believe that some spiritual matters are factually true?

There are two poles of *how* we believe that are measured here. All of us range between:

> *Faithful-Skeptical*

> *Contemplative-Rational*

Are you more *faithfully* inclined or *skeptically* inclined, *contemplatively* inclined or *rationally* inclined? Here is a brief summary of each of the four Spiritual Type possibilities. Read about the type that includes the two poles toward which you tend and see if you agree:

FR: Faithful-Rational

Often the most self-assured and vocal of all the Spiritual Types, the *Faithful-Rational* person believes with great confidence and is ready to explain to naysayers why what (s)he believes is true. FRs usually rest their faith on the promises to be found in scripture and tradition. They often can quote scripture from memory and see scripture as divine truth. The FR's spiritual life is strengthened most through study, and (s)he usually craves conversation with others to stimulate ideas. Often dynamic leaders, FRs can find great benefit in belonging to a religious community and may even see taking a leadership role in one as an obligation.

FC: Faithful-Contemplative

The *Faithful-Contemplative* person believes sometimes even in the face of evidence that (s)he cannot explain away and that (s)he often doesn't care to explain away. Often the most devout and devotional of the Spiritual Types, FCs can be the most dedicated of spiritual practitioners—devoted to daily prayer or meditation, for example. Also the most visionary of the Spiritual Types, FCs believe so strongly in their hearts that they have little interest in dogma or spiritual teaching that seems too intellectual and irrelevant. They can create fascinating spiritual conversations, if you can get them to share their thoughts with you. The FC's relationship to the Divine can sometimes be like a relationship between lovers—intimately personal and also volatile, as FCs can feel at times slighted by the Divine because their relationship is so personal.

SR: Skeptical-Rational

The *Skeptical-Rational* person has little time for spiritual matters. SRs do not believe that dwelling on spiritual things accomplishes much in life. But they often focus on improving the planet, themselves, or their communities with a spiritual zeal. The rarest of the four types, SRs can be very knowledgeable of religion and spiritual traditions, but they do not view that knowledge as offering any evidence for belief. Often the most transitional of the Spiritual Types, many SRs grew up as FRs but have since changed perspectives. Similarly, many SRs go on to become SCs. The most common spiritual practice for SRs is found in their neverending effort to actualize their own full human potential, as well as that of others.

SC: Skeptical-Contemplative

The fastest growing of the Spiritual Types, the *Skeptical-Contemplative* person may not be completely sure what (s)he believes about spiritual things but is interested in discovering what there might be to discover. SCs often do not adhere to any one spiritual tradition exclusively, and they rarely join spiritual groups. They find a variety of spiritual practices and religious traditions stimulating. If they worship, they often do so on their own terms—sometimes participating in religious services but holding on to their own personal convictions in matters of faith. There is an underlying mystical strain in a percentage of SCs as they are intellectually skeptical of all spiritual teaching, but at the same time hold great faith in the guidance of the spirit within them to find the truth.

Tabulate your results for Part Two: Discover Your Tradition Indicator

Step 1

Your responses to the sixty-three statements of Part Two are organized into seven vertical sections. Tabulate the total number of *a*'s and *b*'s for each of the seven sections and enter those totals in the boxes provided, just like you did in tabulating Part One.

Step 2

Next, look at the totals you have written in each of the seven boxes. The highest total determines your results.

Write that letter here: _____

This letter is a key to the spiritual tradition that most closely matches your beliefs. It is a positive indicator of what you believe and what you don't believe—the questions in life that you are asking and trying to answer. This letter represents, in the very broadest of terms, one of seven major spiritual/religious traditions in which your Spiritual Identity will most likely be found. The Tradition Indicators are:

C = Christian Spirituality

B = Buddhist Spirituality

J = Jewish Spirituality

I = Islamic Spirituality

H = Hindu Spirituality

N = New Consciousness Spirituality

U = Humanist Spirituality

You can begin exploring your Spiritual Identity by exploring your Tradition Indicator in all of its many aspects. Keeping in mind your Spiritual Type as well, you can now find resources that will feed your spiritual growth in new ways: people, books, magazines, websites, and spiritual organizations, just to name a few. Chapters 5–7 provide brief summaries of several movements within each of the seven traditions listed above, offering this information for the next stage on your journey.

PART TWO

Setting Out on Your Path

Part Two

Introduction

Your spirituality is within you—you carry it wherever you go. What will you do with yours?

This is where you begin to explore your Spiritual Identity further. The next three chapters contain tools to begin constructing a spiritual life. They contain brief summaries of spiritual traditions readily available in America today, including the spiritual/religious tradition of your Spiritual Identity.

Turn first to the spiritual/religious tradition identified in your results to Part Two of the Spiritual Identity Self-Test. We call this your Tradition Indicator, your *primary* Spiritual Identity. Read it. Hopefully, you will come away with several starting points from which to explore further.

Each brief description contains:

> Basic history and beliefs.

> "People You Should Know" who are representative of the tradition.

> Specific suggestions for further exploration, including

books, magazines, websites, and spiritual organizations of like-minded people.

› Contact information—so that you can find others you might talk with about spirituality and spiritual/religious traditions.

The entries are cross-referenced: wherever an asterisk (*) appears next to mention of a faith tradition, you will be able to find that tradition described in detail elsewhere in Part Two.

Michelangelo was once asked how he would carve an elephant. He replied, "I would take a large piece of stone and take away everything that was not the elephant." Michelangelo's response makes a good analogy for how we can focus on our spiritual lives. Chipping away all that is not an elephant in that great block of stone is like paring away what is not essential to us in order to focus on what is. It is important to know—as you may be beginning this process for the first time—that spiritual growth takes time. You often have to make room in your life for it. You may be disappointed if you simply read about your Spiritual Identity and take it no further. You will find the best results by deepening your understanding further through spiritual practice, reading and study, worship and ritual, and talking with others.

Elizabeth Lesser, cofounder of the Omega Institute, the largest holistic learning center in America, says:

> Not only must we follow the golden thread toward spiritual freedom, but we must also unravel the garden-variety twine that is wrapped tightly around our hearts and minds…. How we unravel the twine—through the hard knocks of daily life and the hard work of self-examination—is just as much a part of the spiritual path as are solitary retreats and meetings with remarkable teachers. In daily life we make real the rarefied wisdom that we can only glean in meditation and in the words of saints and gurus."[1]

Learning from more than one spiritual tradition

Most of us score high on more than one of the seven primary Tradition Indicators in Part Two of the test. Look at your results again to see those *secondary* spiritual traditions that you should also explore. Each of the major seven traditions refers to other spiritual traditions related to it. You will notice these—and, in some cases, suggestions are made for you to turn to them—are based on your Spiritual Type. In these secondary spiritual traditions you may also find tools for spiritual growth.

Each of the twenty-eight faith traditions/spiritual paths represented here has at least 500,000 members and can be found in most parts of North America.

5 ›

Spiritualities Originating in the East

**HINDU SPIRITUALITY · BUDDHIST
SPIRITUALITY · RELATED SPIRITUALITIES**

Hindu Spirituality

With its emphasis on divine union and on the development of God-consciousness in all areas of life, Hinduism is especially appealing to the Contemplative Spiritual Types, SC and FC. Hinduism is difficult to classify in the same way one would other world religions, containing as it does such a vast array of philosophies, beliefs, and practices—as well as millions of individual deities. But there are some things that can be said about Hindu spirituality in general: Hindus generally believe that each individual goes through a cycle of deaths and rebirths (called *samsara*), with the ultimate goal of *moksha*, liberation from the cycle through union with Brahman, the one supreme all-pervading spirit, also known as the Absolute, or God.

The profusion of Hindu gods—from the jovial, elephant-headed Ganesh to the terrifying Kali—are usually seen as manifestations or aspects of the one God. Hindus around the world worship, pray to, and celebrate these deities in a variety of ways.

One's positive deeds and spiritual practices lead to progressively higher rebirths—to situations in life further along the path to union with Brahman. Negative deeds can lead to lower rebirths, even to births in the animal realm. This understanding of the inevitable consequences of one's actions—in this life as well as in the next—is called the law of *karma*.

Within the rich diversity of Hindu practice, there are four basic yogas (literally "yokes"), or paths leading to union with Brahman:

> Jnana Yoga: The path of knowledge, intellectual analysis, and discrimination.

> Karma Yoga: The path of selfless service to others.

> Bhakti Yoga: The path of love and devotion, often expressed through devotion to a particular god or goddess, or *avatar* (incarnation of God) such as Krishna.

> Raja Yoga: Literally "royal" yoga; the scientific approach to liberation, often including physical techniques and practices. Hatha Yoga,* with its practice of bodily postures and breathing techniques, is the form of Raja Yoga most familiar to Westerners.

From the Transcendentalists of New England in the early nineteenth century—including literary figures such as Ralph Waldo Emerson and Henry David Thoreau—through the Beat Movement of the 1950s, and continuing today, many Westerners have been intrigued and influenced by Hinduism. Modern North Americans have incorporated aspects of the Hindu tradition into their lives, particularly through the use of Hatha Yoga* as a physical exercise, but also through a range of practices that demonstrate the rich panoply of Hinduism: from the Integral Yoga of Sri Aurobindo to the devotional chanting of the Hare Krishnas. Though Hinduism's influence outside

India has been significant, few native-born Americans think of themselves as Hindus, even when they adopt Hindu practices. The majority of those who identify themselves as Hindus in America today trace their ethnic origin to the Indian subcontinent.

A Hindu You Should Know: Ramakrishna (1836–1886)

Sri Ramakrishna was born to poor but pious parents in a small village of Bengal, India, and spent the greater part of his fifty years in the Dhaksheswar Temple garden of Calcutta, where he lived in a small hut with his wife, Sri Sarada Devi. He was not a Hindu priest but a lay devotee of the goddess Kali. And though his life was outwardly uneventful, he is an example of someone who cultivated God-consciousness to an amazing degree—to the point of God-intoxication.

He lived in such a state of divine bliss that everyone who met him was immediately drawn to him. People from all walks of life and from all religious traditions flocked to his tiny hut just for the privilege of spending time in his joyous, enlightening presence. His message of divine love created something of a spiritual revival in the India of his day, and his message was later spread to the Western world by his disciple Swami Vivekananda, who lectured and taught extensively in England and the United States. His teachings are contained in the book *The Gospel of Sri Ramakrishna* (Ramakrishna-Vivekananda Center). A good introduction to his teachings is *Selections from the Gospel of Sri Ramakrishna: Annotated and Explained* (SkyLight Paths).

> He who can see the Supreme Lord in all beings, the imperishable amidst the perishable, he it is who really sees.
>
> Beholding the Lord in all things equally, his actions do not mar his spiritual life, but lead him to the height of bliss.
>
> —from the *Bhagavad-gita*, translated by Shri Purohit Swami

Books

Adiswarananda, Swami. *Meditation and Its Practices: A Definitive Guide to Techniques and Traditions of Meditation in Yoga and Vedanta.* Woodstock, Vt.: SkyLight Paths, 2003.

Bhagavad Gita: Annotated and Explained. Translated by Shri Purohit Swami. Annotated by Kendra Crossen Burroughs. Woodstock, Vt.: SkyLight Paths, 2001.

Flood, Gavin D. *An Introduction to Hinduism.* Cambridge: Cambridge University Press, 1996.

Ram Dass. *Be Here Now.* New York: Crown Publishing, 1971.

Viswanathan, Ed. *Am I a Hindu? The Hinduism Primer.*: Halo Books, 1992.

Yogananda, Paramahansa. *The Autobiography of a Yogi.* Los Angeles: Self-Realization Fellowship, 1994.

Periodical

Hinduism Today
107 Kaholalele Rd.
Kapaa, HI 96746-9304
Telephone: (808) 822-7032 ext. 230
Website: www.hinduism-today.com

For More Information

Ramakrishna-Vivekananda Center of New York
17 E. 94th St.
New York, NY 10128
Telephone: (212) 534-9445
Website: www.ramakrishna.org

Sarada Vivekanada Ramakrishna Association
465 Brussels St.
San Francisco, CA 94134
Telephone: (415) 468-4680
Website: www.srv.org

Self-Realization Fellowship
3880 San Rafael Ave.
Los Angeles, CA 90065-3298
Telephone: (323) 225-2471
Website: www.yogananda-srf.org

› Hatha Yoga

Hatha Yoga is the form of yoga with which most Westerners are familiar. *Yoga* literally means "yoke" and can refer to any spiritual practice undertaken as a means to union with the Divine. (The four main classifications of

> Cultivating the feelings of
> friendship, compassion, joy, and equanimity
> toward those who are happy, suffering, worthy,
>   and unworthy,
> purifies consciousness,
> as does the expelling and retaining of the breath.
>
> —from *The Yoga-Sutras of Patanjali*

Hindu yoga are mentioned in the brief description of Hinduism* on page 42). Hatha was originally a part of the Raja Yoga taught by the second-century sage Patanjali, author of the *Yoga-Sutra*. (See *The Yoga-Sutra of Patanjali: A New Translation and Commentary* by Georg Feuerstein, Inner Traditions.) Today it is often thought of— and taught—as a system of bodily exercise, but its original purpose was spiritual: to locate and activate the *chakras*, the centers of spiritual power in the body. Hatha Yoga employs a series of bodily postures as well as control of the breathing to access the *chakras* and to awaken *kundalini*, the spiritual energy that is said to rest dormant in everyone. Those of the SR Spiritual Type—as opposed to SCs, for instance—may want to first explore the non-spiritual side of yoga.

A Hatha Yogi You Should Know: B. K. S. Iyengar (b. 1918)

Belur Krishnamachar Soundaraja Iyengar was born in Karnatka state, India. He was a sickly child, often bedridden, who suffered from a range of diseases, including tuberculosis; he was not expected to live past the age of twenty. In 1934 he met his guru, Sri T. Krishnamacharya, who introduced him to the practice of Hatha Yoga, through which he was restored to vibrant health (he remains vigorous and healthy today in his eighties), and which became for him a spiritual path: "The body is my temple," he often said, "the *asanas* [yoga postures] are my prayers." A renowned teacher of Hatha Yoga, his system is arguably the most influential of the various yogas practiced in America today. His worldwide teaching organization counts thousands of students in more than forty countries.

Books

Feuerstein, Georg. *The Yoga Tradition: Its History, Literature, Philosophy, and Practice*. Prescott, Ariz.: Hohm Press, 1998.

Ittner, John. *Lighting the Lamp of Wisdom: A Week Inside a Yoga Ashram*. Woodstock, Vt.: SkyLight Paths, 2002.

Iyengar, B. K. S. *Light on Yoga*. New York: Schocken Books, 1995.

Kraftsow, Gary. *Yoga for Wellness*. New York: Penguin/Arkana, 1999.

Satchidananda, Swami. *Integral Yoga Hatha*. Buckingham, Va.: Integral Yoga Distribution, 1998.

Periodical

Yoga Journal
2054 University Ave.
Berkeley, CA 94704
Telephone: (510) 841-9200
Website: www.yogajournal.com

For More Information

B. K. S. Iyengar Yoga National Association of the United States
Telephone: (800) 889-9642
Website: www.iyanus.org

The Expanding Light Retreat: Ananda's Retreat Center
14618 Tyler Foote Rd.
Nevada City, CA 95959
Telephone: (800) 346-5350
Website: www.expandinglight.org

Kripalu Center
P.O. Box 793
West St., Route 183
Lenox, MA 01240
Telephone: (800) 741-7353
Website: www.kripalu.org

Satchidananda Ashram-Yogaville
Rte. 1, Box 1720
Buckingham, VA 23921
Telephone: (800) 858-9642
Website: www.yogaville.org

Shree Muktananda Ashram
SYDA Foundation
371 Brickman Rd.
P.O. Box 600
South Fallsburg, NY 12779-0600
Telephone: (845) 434-2000
Website: www.siddhayoga.org

Sivananda Ashram Yoga Ranch Colony
P.O. Box 195
Budd Rd.
Woodbourne, NY 12788
Telephone: (845) 436-6492
Website: www.sivananda.org/ranch

Sivananda Ashram Yoga Retreat
P.O. Box N-7550
Paradise Island, Nassau
Bahamas
Telephone: (800) 783-9642
Website: www.sivananda.org/nassau

Buddhist Spirituality

Buddhism is unique among world religions in that it places no emphasis on belief in, or existence of, a personal God. It is instead concerned with sincere, persistent self-inquiry as a way of perceiving the truth. It has thus attracted the interest of many people with Skeptical Spiritual Types (SRs and SCs) in the West, though FCs, with their mystical bent, are often equally drawn to Buddhist practice.

Buddhism traces its origins to the sixth to fifth centuries BCE in the Himalayan foothills of present-day Nepal, and to the Prince Siddhartha Gautama. Prince Siddhartha, according to the story, grew up in such an extremely protected environment that he knew nothing of the realities of aging, sickness, and death until he was a young man. When he finally did encounter them, he was so overcome that he left his palace and family behind in search of a way of

> The non-doing of any evil,
> the performance of what's skillful,
> the cleansing of one's own mind:
> this is the teaching
> of the Awakened.
>
> —words of the Buddha
> from the *Dhammapada*

liberation, first studying with famous Hindu teachers of the time, and then, when none of them could satisfy his desire, going his own way. One night, seated under the bodhi tree on the banks of the river Neranjara at Bodhgaya, India, he came to understand the true nature of all phenomena: he attained enlightenment. He was thereafter known as the Buddha, the "Awakened One." He spent the rest of his life in teaching. His teaching eventually spread to become a religion prominent throughout large parts of Asia, including China, Japan, Korea, Tibet, and Southeast Asia.

The Buddha's most basic teaching—which is the foundation for all movements within Buddhism—is the Four Noble Truths. They are:

1› The truth of suffering: life is inevitably characterized by suffering, anguish, unsatisfactoriness.

2› The truth of the cause of suffering: the cause is desire.

3› The truth of the eradication of suffering: to eliminate suffering, one must eliminate desire.

4› The truth of the way: desire is eliminated by the practice of the Noble Eightfold Path.

The Noble Eightfold Path consists of the following:

1› Right understanding

2› Right thought

3› Right speech

4› Right action

5› Right livelihood

6› Right effort

7› Right mindfulness

8› Right concentration

Clearly, the Eightfold Path contains enough work for many lifetimes. By putting into practice its principles, one can attain *nirvana*, literally "extinction"—liberation from the cycle of rebirths in which we all find ourselves trapped.

One is usually said to become a Buddhist when one makes a formal act of commitment to the Buddhist practice, called taking refuge in the Three Jewels. The "Three Jewels" referred to are (1) the Buddha, meaning both the historical Buddha and the buddha nature inherent in everyone; (2) the *dharma*, the teachings of the Buddha and also the universal truth to which they point; and (3) the *sangha*, the Buddhist community, sometimes also interpreted as the community of all sentient beings.

In the 2,500 years since the Buddha lived, Buddhism has grown into numerous schools and sects, some of the most prominent of which are described below. All have the Four Noble Truths and the Eightfold Path as a foundation. Almost all emphasize meditation practice. The most common form of meditation—called *Vipassana,* or insight meditation—which is practiced in one way or another by all the schools, involves the focusing of attention for a specified length of time on an object, such as the breath, a particular bodily sensation, or a repeated phrase.

Books

Bercholz, Samuel, and Sherab Chödzin Kohn, eds. *Entering the Stream: An Introduction to the Buddha and His Teachings.* Boston: Shambhala, 1994.

Dhammapada: Annotated and Explained. Translated by Max Müller; revised by Jack Maguire. Annotated by Jack Maguire. Woodstock, Vt.: SkyLight Paths, 2002.

Fields, Rick. *How the Swans Came to the Lake: A Narrative History of Buddhism in America.* Boston: Shambhala Publications, 1995.

Nairn, Rob. *What Is Meditation? Buddhism for Everyone.* Boston: Shambhala Publications, 1999.

Rahula, Walpola. *What the Buddha Taught.* New York: Grove Press, 1986.

Strand, Clark. *Meditation without Gurus: A Guide to the Heart of Practice.* Woodstock, Vt.: SkyLight Paths, 2003.

Periodicals

The Shambhala Sun
1345 Spruce St.
Boulder, CO 80302-9687
Telephone: (902) 422-8404
Website: www.shambhalasun.com

Tricycle: The Buddhist Review
92 Vandam St.
New York, NY 10013
Telephone: (212) 645-1143
Website: www.tricycle.com

> Theravada Spirituality

Theravada (from the Pali for "teaching of the elders") is the name commonly used to refer to the earliest form of Buddhism still in existence, which is practiced extensively throughout Southeast Asia today and is becoming increasingly popular in the West. It is also sometimes known by the somewhat derogatory name Hinayana ("Small Vehicle") in contrast with the later Mahayana ("Great Vehicle") school. In the West, the tradition is frequently known as *Vipassana*, or "insight" meditation—taking its name from one of the key practices.

Theravada Buddhists practice meditation and usually make it part of their daily lives. They also participate in meditation retreats, consisting of one or more days and up to several months. Some practice a form of meditation called *metta*, which consists of directing the intention of love and well-being toward oneself and all other beings. Chanting of the Buddhist sutras is another common practice.

> What we are is the result of what we have thought,
> is built by our thoughts, is made up of our thoughts.
> If one speaks or acts with an impure thought,
> suffering follows one,
> like the wheel of the cart follows the foot of the ox.
>
> What we are is the result of what we have thought,
> is built by our thoughts, is made up of our thoughts.
> If one speaks or acts with a pure thought,
> happiness follows one,
> like a shadow that never leaves.
>
> —words of the Buddha from the *Dhammapada*

Theravada Buddhists usually regard as scripture the Pali canon, or *Tripitaka*, the recorded sayings and acts of the Buddha that were transcribed from the oral tradition within a few generations of his death (a portion of which is available in a good English translation as *The Middle-Length Discourses of the Buddha*, translated by Bhikku Bodhi and Bhikku Nanamoli [Wisdom Publications] and *The Long Discourses of the Buddha*, translated by Maurice Walshe [Wisdom Publications]). Adherence to the Four Noble Truths and the Noble Eightfold Path is especially strong among Theravadins.

A Theravada Buddhist You Should Know:
Joseph Goldstein (b. 1944)

Joseph Goldstein first became interested in Buddhism while a young Peace Corps volunteer in Thailand in the 1960s. He was a member, along with his teaching colleagues Jack Kornfield and Sharon Salzberg, of the first group of Americans to study extensively with the renowned Buddhist teachers of the "Forest Tradition" of Thailand and Burma, including Anagarika Munindra, S. N. Goenka, Dipa Ma, and the Venerable U Pandita Sayadaw. He has been one of the primary teachers of that tradition in the Western world, leading insight and lovingkindess meditation retreats worldwide since 1974. He is a cofounder of the Insight Meditation Society in Barre, Massachusetts, where he is one of the guiding teachers. In 1989, together with several other teachers and students, he helped establish the Barre Center for Buddhist Studies. He is the author of *One Dharma: The Emerging Western Buddhism* (HarperSanFrancisco), *The Experience of Insight: A Simple and Direct Guide to Buddhist Meditation* (Shambhala Publications), *Insight Meditation: The Practice of Freedom* (Shambhala Publications), and coauthor (with Jack Kornfield) of *Seeking the Heart of Wisdom: The Path of Insight Meditation* (Shambhala Publications).

Books

Gunaratana, Venerable Henepola. *Mindfulness in Plain English*. Boston: Wisdom Publications, 1993.

Rosenberg, Larry. *Breath by Breath: The Liberating Practice of Insight Meditation*. Boston: Shambhala Publications, 1998.

Salzberg, Sharon. *Lovingkindness: The Revolutionary Art of Happiness*. Boston: Shambhala Publications, 1997.

For More Information

The Bhavana Society
Route 1, Box 218–3
High View, WV 26808
Telephone: (304) 856-3241
Website: www.bhavanasociety.org

The Insight Meditation Society
1230 Pleasant St.
Barre, MA 01005
Telephone: (978) 355-4378
Website: www.dharma.org

Spirit Rock Meditation Center
P.O. Box 169
Woodacre, CA 94973
Telephone: (415) 488-0164
Website: www.spiritrock.org

› Zen Spirituality

Zen is the best-known form of the school of Buddhism known as Mahayana, the "Great Vehicle." Mahayana Buddhism is distinguishable from earlier schools in its emphasis on the enlightened nature inherent in all beings—an enlightenment that needs to be *discovered* rather than attained—and on its teaching of the essential emptiness of all we perceive. The Mahayana is also characterized by the importance of *bodhisattvas* ("enlightenment beings"), mythic or symbolic figures who vow to postpone their own enlightenment until they have helped all other sentient beings become enlightened as well. They are models for the kind of selfless compassion to which Zen students aspire. The Mahayana also accepts scriptures of much later origin than the *Tripitaka*, such as the Prajnaparamita ("perfection of wisdom") sutras (for selections from the Prajnaparamita literature with commentary, see *The Diamond That Cuts Through Illusion* by Thich Nhat Hanh [Parallax Press] and *Zen and the Art of Insight* by Thomas Cleary [Shambhala Publications]).

Zen students, like other Buddhists, place great importance upon meditation, both daily and in longer retreats. Zen students also practice chanting, almost always of the Mahayana scriptures, especially the Heart Sutra. Zen meditation retreats are characterized by greater formality than Theravada ones, with every aspect of the schedule—including meals—operating according to a strict system of movement and behavior. Students of the Rinzai and Korean schools of Zen also work with *koans*, unsolvable questions designed to take the student beyond the limits of rational thought—"What is the sound of one hand clapping?" is perhaps the most famous example.

Still widely practiced in China, Korea, and Japan, Zen has had a significant presence and

> The Great Way is not difficult
> for those who have no preferences.
> When love and hate are both absent
> everything becomes clear and undisguised.
> Make the smallest distinction, however,
> and heaven and earth are set infinitely apart.
> If you wish to see the truth
> then hold no opinions for or against anything.
> To set up what you like against what you dislike
> is the disease of the mind.
> When the deep meaning of things is not understood
> the mind's essential peace is disturbed to no avail.
>
> —from the *Hsin Hsin Ming* ("Verses on Faith-Mind") by Sengstan (sixth century CE)

influence in the United States since the 1950s, when it was explored and adopted by members of the Beat generation.

A Zen Buddhist You Should Know:
Shunryu Suzuki (1904–1971)

Shunryu Suzuki-roshi, a Japanese Zen master belonging to the Soto lineage, came to San Francisco in 1959 at the age of fifty-four to serve the Japanese Buddhist community in California. But he was so impressed with the seriousness and quality of "beginner's mind" among the Americans who sought him as a teacher that he decided to stay in the United States to teach Zen to them. Many of the first generation of native-born American Zen teachers are his students, and he is among the most influential of all the teachers who brought Zen to America. Some of Suzuki-roshi's edited talks were collected in the book *Zen Mind, Beginner's Mind* (Weatherhill), which has become a modern classic, read and reread by American Zen students since its first appearance. A second collection of his talks, *Branching Streams Flow in the Darkness* (University of California Press) was also published, and he is the subject of the biography *Crooked Cucumber* by David Chadwick (Broadway Books).

Books

Aitken, Robert. *Taking the Path of Zen*. Berkeley, Calif.: North Point Press, 1985.

Beck, Charlotte Joko. *Everyday Zen*. San Francisco: HarperSanFrancisco, 1989.

Herrigel, Eugen. *Zen in the Art of Archery*. New York: Random House, 1999.

Kapleau, Philip, ed. *The Three Pillars of Zen: Teaching, Practice, and Enlightenment*. New York: Anchor/Doubleday, 1989.

Maguire, Jack. *Waking Up: A Week Inside a Zen Monastery*. Woodstock, Vt.: SkyLight Paths, 2000.

Nhat Hanh, Thich. *Peace Is Every Step: The Path of Mindfulness in Everyday Life.* Edited by Arnold Kotler. New York: Bantam, 1992.
Seung Sahn. *Dropping Ashes on the Buddha: The Teaching of Zen Master Seung Sahn.* Edited by Stephen Mitchell. New York: Grove Press, 1994.
Young, Andi. *The Sacred Art of Bowing: Preparing to Practice.* Woodstock, Vt.: SkyLight Paths, 2003.

Periodical

Primary Point
99 Pound Rd.
Cumberland, RI 02864
Telephone: (401) 658-1476
Website: www.kwanumzen.com/ppp

For More Information

Green Mountain Dharma Center (for women)
P.O. Box 182
Hartland Four Corners, VT 05049
Telephone: (802) 436-1103/1102
Maple Forest Monastery (for men)
P.O. Box 354
South Woodstock, VT 05071
Telephone: (802) 457-9442

The Kwan Um School of Zen
99 Pound Rd.
Cumberland, RI 02864
Telephone: (401) 658-1464
Website: www.kwanumzen.com

Mount Baldy Zen Center
P.O. Box 429
Mount Baldy, CA 91759
Telephone: (909) 985-6410
Website: www.mbzc.org

Plum Village
Upper Hamlet (for men)
Le Pey, 24240
Thenac, France
Telephone: 33-5-53-58-48-58
Lower Hamlet (for women)
Meyrac, 47120
Loubes-Bernac, France
Telephone: 33-5-53-94-75-40
Website: www.plumvillage.org

San Francisco Zen Center
300 Page St.
San Francisco, CA 94102
Telephone: (415) 863-3136
Website: www.sfzc.com

Zen Mountain Monastery
P.O. Box 197
Mount Tremper, NY 12457
Telephone: (845) 688-2228
Website: www.zen-mtn.org

› Nichiren Spirituality

Nichiren Buddhism is one of the most popular modern manifestations of the type of Buddhism known as "Pure Land," a movement of the Mahayana school. It is also the type of Buddhism most appealing to the Faithful (FR and FC) Spiritual Types. The objective in Pure Land practices is usually to place one's faith in the *bodhisattva* ("enlightening being") named Amida, or Amitabha, in hope of being born in the next life into an existence in the "Pure Land," where conditions are extremely conducive to enlightenment (unlike our present world, where conditions are so difficult that enlightenment can take many lifetimes).

The Nichiren sect was named for its founder, the former Zen monk Nichiren (1222–1282) in part as a reaction to the official Buddhism prevalent in Japan at the time, whose practice was complicated and accessible mostly to the monastic elite. Nichiren's movement opened up the possibility of Buddhist practice to one and all—men and women, lay and monastic alike.

The principle Nichiren Buddhist practice is the chanting of the mantra *nam-myoho-renge-kyo* ("hail to the Lotus Sutra") morning and evening in front of a home shrine, the *gohonzon*. Nichiren Buddhists also gather to practice chanting together. Nichiren Buddhism is unique in that it places an emphasis on material prosperity as something that naturally arises for the one who chants *nam-myoho-renge-kyo*, just as enlightenment does. The worldwide Nichiren organization called Soka Gakkai International has many regional centers throughout the United States.

> Life flashes by in but a moment. No matter how many terrible enemies we may encounter, banish all fears and never think of backsliding. Even if someone were to cut off our heads with a saw, impale us with lances, or shackle our feet and bore them through with a gimlet, as long as we are alive, we must keep chanting *Nam-myoho-renge-kyo, Nam-myoho-renge-kyo.*
>
> —Nichiren Daishonin, founder of the Nichiren School

Books

Hammond, Phillip E. and David W. MacHacek. *Soka Gakkai in America: Accommodation and Conversion.* Oxford: Oxford Univ. Press, 1999.

Metraux, Daniel A. *The Soka Gakkai Revolution.* Lanham, Md.: University Press of America, 1994.

Yampolsky, Philip, ed. *Nichiren: Selected Writings of Nichiren.* Translated by Burton Watson. New York: Columbia University Press, 1990.

Periodical

Living Buddhism
SGI USA Subscriptions Department
P.O. Box 1427
Santa Monica, CA 90406-1427
Telephone: (800) 835-4558

For More Information

Soka Gakkai International—USA Headquarters
SGI Plaza
606 Wilshire Blvd.
Santa Monica, CA 90401
Telephone: (310) 260-8900
Website: www.sgi-usa.org

› Tibetan Spirituality

Tibetan Buddhism has recently become very popular in the West through the teachings of such figures as Lama Surya Das, Pema Chö-drön, Sogyal Rinpoche, and, of course, the Dalai Lama. Also sometimes known as *Vajrayana* ("Diamond Vehicle"), or Tantric Buddhism, this school has been taught and practiced outside Tibet and North India mainly since the 1970s. It developed out of the Mahayana teachings in northwest India around 500 CE and spread to Tibet, China, and Japan. For several hundred years it has been the chief form of Buddhism practiced in the Himalayan region. Tibetan Buddhists use scriptures that are of even more recent origin than the Mahayana sutras. Some of them are actually considered to be quite ancient in origin but were thought to have been kept hidden until the time was ripe for their revelation.

In addition to meditation practices similar to those used by the other Buddhist schools, Tibetan practice involves esoteric visualization methods, rituals, and the repetition of *mantras*—practices that are usually transferred formally through a ceremony of initiation. Relationship with a teacher is critically important in Tibetan Buddhism, as many of the practices can be learned only through a teacher and can even be counterproductive if not undertaken under a teacher's careful guidance. The strong devotion to teachers which is characteristic of Tibetan Buddhism is called "guru yoga." All four Spiritual Types are common in Tibetan Buddhism.

> All worldly pursuits have but the one unavoidable end, which is sorrow: acquisitions end in dispersion; buildings in destruction; meetings in separation; births, in death. Knowing this, one should, from the very first, renounce acquisition and heaping up, and building, and meeting; and faithful to the commands of an eminent guru, set about realizing the Truth (which has no birth or death).
>
> —from the Tibetan scripture
> *The Hundred Thousand Songs of Milarepa*

A Tibetan Buddhist You Should Know:
The Fourteenth Dalai Lama (b. 1935)

Tenzin Gyatso, His Holiness the Fourteenth Dalai Lama, is the spiritual and temporal leader of the six million Tibetan people. He was born Lhamo Dhondup in a small village in northeastern Tibet and was recognized at the age of two to be the reincarnation of his predecessor, the Thirteenth Dalai Lama. As political as well as religious leader of Tibet, he sought a peaceful reconciliation with the Chinese, who occupied his country in the 1950s, but was finally forced to flee in 1959, setting up a government in exile in Dharamsala, India. Eighty thousand Tibetan refugees followed him. He promulgated a democratic constitution, based on Buddhist principles, and the Universal Declaration of Human Rights, as a model for a future free Tibet.

Known for his joyful, compassionate presence, the Dalai Lama has been greatly responsible for the rise in interest in Tibetan Buddhism, and of Buddhism of all kinds, in our time. He is the author of several best-selling books, including *The Art of Happiness: A Handbook for Living* (Riverhead) and *Ethics for the New Millennium* (Riverhead).

Books

Chödrön, Pema. *The Wisdom of No Escape: And the Path of Loving-Kindness*. Boston: Shambhala, 1991.

Das, Lama Surya. *Awakening the Buddha Within: Tibetan Wisdom for the Western World*. New York: Broadway Books, 1998.

Sogyal Rinpoche. *The Tibetan Book of Living and Dying*. San Francisco: HarperSanFrancisco, 1994.

Thurman, Robert A. F. *Essential Tibetan Buddhism*. San Francisco: HarperSanFrancisco, 1996.

Trungpa, Chögyam. *Shambhala: The Sacred Path of the Warrior*. Boston: Shambhala Publications, 1988.

For More Information

Gampo Abbey
Pleasant Bay, Nova Scotia
Canada B0E 2P0
Telephone: (902) 224-2752
Website: www.gampoabbey.org

Karmê Chöling Buddhist Meditation Center
369 Patneaude Lane
Barnet, VT 05821
Telephone: (802) 633-2384
Website: www.kcl.shambhala.org

Rigpa International
449 Powell St., Suite 200
San Francisco, CA 94102
Telephone: (415) 392-2055
Website: www.rigpa.org

Rocky Mountain Shambhala Center
4921 County Rd. 68-C
Red Feather Lakes, CO 80545
Telephone: (970) 881-2184
Website: www.rmsc.shambhala.org

6›

Spiritualities Most Common in the West

JEWISH SPIRITUALITY · CHRISTIAN SPIRITUALITY · ISLAMIC SPIRITUALITY · RELATED SPIRITUALITIES

Jewish Spirituality

All Jewish spirituality centers on Torah, the accumulation of several thousand years of Jewish wisdom. As Rabbi Lawrence A. Hoffman, a leading authority on prayer and liturgy, describes it, Torah "is synonymous with learning, wisdom, and love of God. Without it, life has neither meaning nor value." Usually identified with the first five books in the Bible (the Five Books of Moses), Torah, in a larger sense, means "way of life." If Judaism is the spiritual tradition that best matches your Spiritual Identity you will find that the purpose of life and meaning of God find their supreme expression in Torah.

Judaism is one of the more difficult of spiritualities to describe easily. It is a living tradition that includes religious rituals and beliefs as well as a code of ethical behavior. It also incorporates and reflects the ancient and modern history of the Jews as a people with rituals, ceremonies, and celebrations. Its adherents today include people of every race and most nations—and every Spiritual Type.

Several movements exist within Judaism today, and each represents a particular attitude toward ritual, liturgy, theology and tradition. Each movement ordains rabbis ("teachers," or spiritual leaders) and has temples or synagogues in all major cities in North America.

An important belief in Orthodox Judaism is that the Torah used today is the same as the Torah that was given to Moses on Mount Sinai; as divine revelation, its requirements are not meant to be reinterpreted in any fundamental way in light of later events. The other three Jewish movements view a human component as being present in Torah, thus making it valid to reinterpret Torah for each era. Each of these three movements—Conservative, Reconstructionist, and Reform—places different emphases on the important Jewish concepts of God, Torah, and Israel (the Jewish community).

> Hear, O Israel! The Lord is our God, the Lord alone. You shall love the Lord your God with all your heart and with all your soul and with all your might. Take to heart these instructions with which I charge you this day. Impress them upon your children. Recite them when you stay at home and when you are away, when you lie down and when you get up. Bind them as a sign on your hand and let them serve as a symbol on your forehead; inscribe them on the doorposts of your house and on your gates.
>
> —Deuteronomy 6:4–9: from the *Sh'ma*, the Jewish affirmation of faith

A Jew You Should Know:
Abraham Joshua Heschel (1907–1972)

Abraham Joshua Heschel was born in Poland, a descendant of a long line of rabbis of the mystically inclined Hasidim, a spiritual movement within Judaism that began in Eastern Europe in the early eighteenth century. He studied Talmud, Hasidic teachings, and kabbalah as a youth, and attended the University of Berlin. Emigrating from Nazi Germany in 1938, he ultimately settled in the United States, where he became professor at Hebrew Union College in Cincinnati and then at the Jewish Theological Seminary of America in New York. Heschel taught that God is passionately concerned with all creation, and the nature of true religion is humanity's response to God's bond with it. The root of Jewish observance is in human response expressed with love and devotion. One of Heschel's most beloved books, his 1951 *The Sabbath* (Noonday Press), focuses on the holiness of time, an important principle for all Judaism. Since Judaism had not given the world any holy places outside the Land of Israel—such as special temples or enormous cathedrals—he wrote, its Sabbath and various holidays created palaces in time, temporal refuges from the pressures of the world.

Books

Cohen, Norman J. *The Way Into Torah.* Woodstock, Vt.: Jewish Lights Publishing, 2000.

Gillman, Neil. *Sacred Fragments: Recovering Theology for the Modern Jew.* Philadelphia: The Jewish Publication Society, 1990.

———. *The Way Into Encountering God in Judaism.* Woodstock, Vt.: Jewish Lights Publishing, 2000.

Green, Arthur. *These Are the Words: A Vocabulary of Jewish Spiritual Life.* Woodstock, Vt.: Jewish Lights Publishing, 1999.

Heschel, Abraham Joshua. *The Sabbath.* New York: Noonday Press, 1996.

Hoffman, Lawrence A. *The Way Into Jewish Prayer.* Woodstock, Vt.: Jewish Lights Publishing, 2000.

Kertzer, Rabbi Morris N. *What Is a Jew?* Revised by Rabbi Lawrence A. Hoffman. New York: Macmillan, 1993.

Kushner, Lawrence. *The Book of Letters: A Mystical Hebrew Alphabet.* Woodstock, Vt.: Jewish Lights Publishing, 1990.

———. *Jewish Spirituality: A Brief Introduction for Christians.* Woodstock, Vt.: Jewish Lights Publishing, 2001.

———. *The Way Into Jewish Mystical Tradition.* Woodstock, Vt.: Jewish Lights Publishing, 2001.

Matlins, Stuart M., ed. *The Jewish Lights Spirituality Handbook: A Guide to Understanding, Exploring and Living a Spiritual Life.* Woodstock, Vt.: Jewish Lights Publishing, 2001.

Olitzky, Kerry M., and Daniel Judson. *The Rituals and Practices of a Jewish Life: A Handbook for Personal Spiritual Renewal.* Woodstock, Vt.: Jewish Lights Publishing, 2002.

Wouk, Herman. *This Is My God: The Jewish Way of Life.* New York: Little, Brown & Co., 1992.

Periodicals

Lilith
The Independent Jewish Women's Magazine
250 W. 57th St., Suite 2432
New York, NY 10107
Telephone: (888) 254-5484
Website: www.lilithmag.com

Moment: The Magazine of Jewish Culture and Opinion
P.O. Box 7028
Red Oak, IA 51591
Telephone: (800) 777-1005
Website: www.momentmag.com

Tikkun: A Bimonthly Jewish Critique of Politics,
  Culture, and Society
P.O. Box 460926
Escondido, CA 92046
Telephone: (800) 395-7753
Website: www.tikkun.org

For More Information

To find a synagogue (also often called *shul*, or "temple") near you, look in your phone book. Listings will often note whether the synagogue is a member of the Reform, Conservative, Reconstructionist, or Orthodox movements. Others may be noted as "interdenominational." Otherwise, you may call ahead and ask.

Aleph: Alliance for Jewish Renewal
7000 Lincoln Dr. B2
Philadelphia, PA 19119
Telephone: (215) 247-9700
Website: www.aleph.org

Jewish Reconstructionist Federation
Beit Devora
7804 Montgomery Ave., Suite 9
Elkins Park, PA 19027-2649
Telephone: (215) 782-8500
Website: www.jrf.org

Union for Reform Judaism
633 Third Ave.
New York, NY 10017-6778
Telephone: (212) 650-4000
Website: www.uahc.org

Union of Orthodox Jewish Congregations
11 Broadway
New York, NY 10004
Telephone: (212) 563-4000
Website: www.ou.org

United Synagogue of Conservative Judaism
155 Fifth Ave.
New York, NY 10010-6802
Telephone: (212) 533-7800
Website: www.uscj.org

Christian Spirituality

All Christian spiritualities are based on the person of Jesus Christ and his message, as it is recorded in the four Gospels of the New Testament. Christian tradition looks to the events of Jesus' life, his death, and his resurrection from the dead as literally true. Christians believe that Jesus was God in the form of a human being, and that he came into the world to liberate all people from the bondage to sin that is the common human condition. For the Faithful (FR and FC) Spiritual Types, this Jesus of history is the foundation for faith. In contrast, Skeptical (SR and SC) Spiritual Types often find meaning in the life of Jesus that does not rely upon a literal interpretation of the events of the Gospels.

> "I am the way, the truth, and the life."
>
> —words of Jesus, in John 14:6

The many Christian movements and denominations found today can all be located within the related traditions of Catholicism,* Eastern Orthodoxy,* and Protestantism.* The early Christian Church was somewhat loosely organized in its early centuries and became a unified system only in the fourth century, when the emperor Constantine gave Christianity favored status in the Roman Empire. What then became a unified church was split in two in the eleventh century, when its eastern and western regions reached an impasse over theological issues. The Western Church is known today as the Roman Catholic Church, with its ecclesiastical center in Rome (there are Eastern Catholic Churches as well); the Eastern is known today as the Eastern Orthodox Church, with its center in Constantinople (present-day Istanbul, Turkey). In the early sixteenth century, Martin Luther, a German Roman Catholic monk, led a protest against the Catholic Church's abuses of authority that resulted in a further split in the Western Church. Luther's movement—and the rich variety of denominations and movements it engendered—became known as Protestantism.*

Christians are for the most part united in their unique belief in God as Trinity: that one God exists in the form of three distinct persons, the Father, the Son (Jesus Christ), and the Holy Spirit. For nearly every Christian group, initiation into the Church, the Christian community, is accomplished through baptism, though the form of the rite varies greatly—from sprinkling with water to total immersion of the body in it. Most Christians also commemorate, in one form or another, the last meal Jesus ate with his disciples before his crucifixion, the Last Supper (sometimes called the "Holy Eucharist" or "Holy Communion").

The Christian Bible is composed of the Hebrew Scriptures, which Christians often call the Old Testament, and the series of books and letters written in Greek within one hundred and fifty years of Jesus' death, called the New Testament. Catholic and Eastern Orthodox Bibles contain several books that Protestant Bibles do not.

Contemplation of the words of Jesus, focus on the person of Jesus, study of the meaning of Jesus' life, death, and resurrection, and praying to Jesus are spiritual practices common among Christians.

› Roman Catholic Spirituality

The Catholic interpretation of biblical history and doctrine is usually literal. Even so, there has been a rise in the number of Skeptical Spiritual Types among Catholics, particularly in the years since the 1960s, when the Church officially embraced a somewhat more open and ecumenical attitude in matters of doctrine, worship, and in the relationship of the Catholic Church to other faith traditions.

Catholic spirituality focuses on the celebration of the Eucharist, or the Mass—the rite of thanksgiving that commemorates Jesus' last meal with his disciples. In the Eucharist, bread and wine are blessed by the priest celebrating the Mass, at which point they are said to become the body and blood of Christ. When Catholics receive the consecrated bread and wine (or, often, only the bread) they are taking Christ into themselves in this special way, as the supreme form of spiritual nourishment. The Mass is the principal worship service of the Catholic Church, and attendance at it on Sundays is an obligation for Catholics. For this reason Catholic churches usually offer more than one celebration of the Mass each Sunday—sometimes many. Most churches (also called parishes) also offer masses on a daily basis.

Catholics regard the pope, who is the bishop of Rome, to be the head of the Church on Earth. Since the Catholic Church is the largest of all Christian bodies (with nearly a billion members worldwide), the pope is also one of the most influential religious leaders in the world. The Catholic Church traces the continuity of its tradition back to the time of Jesus himself, and its hierarchy to the twelve disciples he appointed. It is believed that the Apostle Peter, one of Jesus' original twelve, was the first bishop (literally "overseer") of the Christian community of Rome.

The Prayer of St. Francis of Assisi

Lord, make me an instrument of your peace:
Where there is hatred let me sow love,
Where there is injury, pardon;
Where there doubt, faith;
Where there is despair, hope;
Where there is darkness, light;
Where there is sadness, joy;
O Divine Master, grant that I may not so much seek:
   to be consoled, as to console;
   to be understood, as to understand;
   to be loved as to love.
For it is in giving that we receive, it is in pardoning that we are pardoned.
And it is in dying that we are born to Eternal Life.
Amen

The veneration of saints—people who have been judged by the Church to be especially holy—is a practice for many Catholics. The saints are role models of a kind, and Catholics pray to them, asking for their guidance and for their intercession with God. Among the saints, the Virgin Mary, Jesus' mother, occupies a special place. It is a dogma of the Church that Mary was immaculately conceived; that is, that her conception occurred in a miraculous way that kept her pure from the condition of original sin into which all other humans are born.

Also central to Catholic spirituality are seven sacraments, means of God's grace administered by the Church: baptism, confirmation, reconciliation, the Eucharist, marriage, holy orders (ordination to the priesthood or profession as a monk or nun), and anointing of the sick. Other Catholic spiritual practices include *lectio divina* ("spiritual reading") and centering prayer, which is a kind of silent meditation.

A Catholic You Should Know: Mother Teresa (1919–1998)

Agnes Gonxha Bojaxhiu, who became Mother Teresa of Calcutta, was born in Macedonia. At age eighteen she joined the Sisters of Loreto, a Roman Catholic teaching order, and was sent to teach at a school for girls in Calcutta, India. The sight of huge numbers of the ill and dying on Calcutta's streets moved her deeply, and she became convinced of her calling to help care for them. In 1950, Pope Pius XII granted her request to establish a new order of nuns, the Missionaries of Charity, and she and her sisters began the work of caring for the destitute and dying for which they have become famous throughout the world. Mother Teresa was a fervent advocate of the right-to-life movement, and a firm supporter of papal policies. She was awarded the 1979 Nobel Peace Prize. Her books include *The Best Gift Is Love* (Servant Publications). In 2003 she was beatified by Pope John Paul II, a significant step toward sainthood in the Roman Catholic Church.

Books

Aprile, Dianne. *Making a Heart for God: A Week Inside a Catholic Monastery*. Woodstock, Vt.: SkyLight Paths, 2001.

The Essential Catholic Handbook: A Summary of Beliefs, Practices, and Prayers. Liguori, Mo.: Liguori Publications, 1997.

Foley, Leonard. *Believing in Jesus: A Popular Overview of the Catholic Faith*. Cincinnati: St. Anthony Messenger Press, 1995.

John Paul II, Pope. *Catechism of the Catholic Church*. San Francisco: Ignatius Press, 1994.

———. *Pope John Paul II: In My Own Words*. New York: Gramercy, 2002.

McBrien, Richard P., Harold W. Attridge and Theodore M Hesburgh, eds. *The HarperCollins Encyclopedia of Catholicism*. San Francisco: HarperSanFrancsico, 1995.

Pennington, M. Basil. *Centering Prayer: Renewing an Ancient Christian Prayer Form*. New York: Image Books, 1982.

Pennington, M. Basil, Thomas Keating, and Thomas E. Clarke. *Finding Grace at the Center: The Beginning of Centering Prayer*. Woodstock, Vt.: SkyLight Paths, 2002.

Rupp, Joyce. *The Cup of Life: A Guide for Spiritual Growth*. Notre Dame, Ind.: Ave Maria Press, 1997.

For More Information

Roman Catholic churches, or parishes, are easily found throughout the United States. For further information about the Catholic faith, you may contact one of the organizations below.

Catholic Information Center on the Internet
Website: www.catholic.net

Catholic Online
Catholic news, message boards, and links to other Catholic organizations and groups.
Website: www.catholic.org

United States Conference of Catholic Bishops
3211 Fourth St., NE
Washington, D.C. 20017-1194

Telephone: (202) 541-3000
Website: www.nccbuscc.org

> > Liberation Spirituality

With its emphasis on action motivated by faith, this Christian spirituality is quite common among Faithful Spiritual Types. *Liberation theology* is a term that arose in the mid-twentieth century to describe the efforts of Latin American theologians to make the Christian message relevant to the oppressive social, economic, and political situation experienced by the people of Latin America. In a direct challenge to the existing situation in which established churches used Christian doctrine to support oppressive political regimes, Liberation theologians saw in Jesus' life a message of liberation for the oppressed of all kinds.

Liberation theologians read the New Testament in a way that speaks to specific people living under specific conditions at specific moments in history. The Liberation approach has since been used in the work of such activists as James H. Cone, who has articulated theology from an African-American perspective; the gay rights activist Gary David Comstock; South Africa's Archbishop Desmond Tutu; and by Palestinian Christians in Israel like Father Elias Chacour.

> Poverty is an act of love and liberation. It has a redemptive value. If the ultimate cause of human exploitation and alienation is selfishness, the deepest reason for voluntary poverty is love of neighbor. Christian poverty has meaning only as a commitment of solidarity with the poor, with those who suffer misery and injustice. The commitment is to witness to the evil which has resulted from sin and is a breach of communion. It is not a question of idealizing poverty, but rather of taking it on as it is—an evil—to protest against it and to struggle to abolish it.
>
> —Gustavo Gutierrez, *A Theology of Liberation*

A Liberation Theologian You Should Know:
Oscar Romero (1917–1980)

In February 1977, three weeks after Oscar Romero was consecrated archbishop of Santiago de Maria, El Salvador, his friend, the Jesuit priest Rutilio Grande, was victim of a politically motivated assassination. The event was, for Romero, a conversion. He began a ministry of outspoken commitment to those who had no voice of their own, which eventually led to his speaking out against the government on behalf of the people, by whom he was held in the highest regard. When Pope John Paul II asked him not to deal with the specifics of the oppression against which he so often spoke, but to speak of general principles, Romero replied that specific murders in El Salvador were not adequately dealt with by stating general principles. The Vatican attempted to appoint an administrator to oversee his work, but he was killed before this could be put into effect. He was assassinated while celebrating the Mass in the chapel of the Divine Providence Hospital, where he lived. He remains a hero among Salvadorans as well as with others throughout the world.

Books

Andelson, Robert V. *From Wasteland to Promised Land: Liberation Theology for a Post-Modern World.* Maryknoll, N.Y.: Orbis Books, 1992.

Brown, Robert McAfee. *Liberation Theology: An Introductory Guide.* Louisville, Ky.:Westminster John Knox Press, 1993.

Chacour, Elias. *Blood Brothers.* Fairfax, Va.: Chosen Books, 1971.

Guttiérez, Gustavo. *Gustavo Guttiérez: Essential Writings,* edited by James B. Nickoloff. Maryknoll, N.Y.: Orbis Books, 1996.

———. *A Theology of Liberation: History, Politics, and Salvation.* Maryknoll, N.Y.: Orbis Books, 1971.

Romero, Oscar. *The Violence of Love.* Translated by James R. Brockman, S.J. Farmington, Pa.: Plough Publishing House, 1998.

Periodical

Sojourners
2401 15th St. NW
Washington, D.C. 20009
Telephone: (800) 714-7474
Website: www.sojourners.com

For More Information

There is no specific organization in the United States that represents Liberation Spirituality, although college courses are offered on the subject and many American clergy incorporate its ideas in their preaching and work. An organization that has inspired many Catholic men and women to dedicate their lives to the principles of Liberation Spirituality in Latin America is the Catholic Foreign Mission Society of America, known as Maryknoll. They can be contacted at:

Maryknoll Mission Association of the Faithful
P.O. Box 307
Maryknoll, NY 10545-0307
Telephone: (800) 818-5276
Website: home.maryknoll.org

› Protestant Spirituality

The spirituality of Protestants is most often centered around the Bible—reading it, studying it, and using it as a guide for life. Martin Luther's original principle is still very much alive among Protestants today: that each person has the God-given inner resources to understand the meaning of the scriptures on his or her own. Protestants believe that each Christian has a direct relationship with God and can communicate with God with no kind of human intermediary needed. They are united in the belief that Jesus' death on the cross made him the only necessary intermediary between God and humanity. This belief finds expression in the traditions of Protestant prayer: many Protestants will consistently conclude their prayers "in the name of Jesus."

Protestant spirituality is distinctively independent, which explains why there are so many denominations, or different church traditions, within it. All Spiritual Types can be found within Protestantism—the Skeptical and Contemplative Types most often found within Mainline Protestantism* and Faithful Types more often in Evangelical Protestantism.*

> As many of us as have been baptized are all priests...which is a far greater thing than being kings, for priesthood makes us worthy to stand before God.
>
> —Martin Luther

All Protestants use the same Bible. The Protestant canon of scriptures excludes several books found in Catholic and Orthodox Bibles that are sometimes known collectively as the Apocrypha. Protestant worship includes prayers, the singing of hymns, readings from the Bible, and sermons based on readings. Protestant spiritual practices run the gamut from the rich liturgy and daily cycle of prayer of the Episcopalians to the simple and austere religious meetings of the Quakers.*

A Protestant You Should Know: Dietrich Bonhoeffer (1906–1945)

Dietrich Bonhoeffer was one of the first pastors in Nazi Germany to recognize the Christian responsibility for Nazi persecution of the Jews. Born in Germany, he studied at Union Theological Seminary in New York and the University of Berlin, where he taught through the early and mid-1930s. In his teaching, he addressed the causes of the alienation between Judaism* and Christianity,* and showed that efforts to curtail the theological significance of the Jewish heritage must be regarded as heretical. He was continually disappointed by the timidity of the confessing Church in helping the Jews. In 1942 he was arrested for smuggling fifteen Jews into Switzerland, and was implicated in a plot to assassinate Hitler. He was hanged in the concentration camp at Flossenburg on April 9, 1945. His most popular books include *Letters and Meditations from Prison* (Macmillan) and *The Cost of Discipleship* (Simon & Schuster).

›› Mainline Protestantism

Mainline Protestantism takes its name from the so-called mainline churches, or those that represent the oldest movements within Protestantism, including: Episcopalian or Anglican, Lutheran, Presbyterian, Mennonite,* and Methodist churches; and in Canada, the United Church of Canada.

Mainline Protestants focus on reinterpreting the Bible for each era, with the goal of ensuring that it speaks relevantly to modern concerns. Most Mainline Protestant churches, for instance, in contrast to Evangelical Protestant churches, ordain women as clergy, and some ordain gay men and lesbians as well.

> For by grace you have been saved through faith; and this is not your own doing, it is the gift of God—not because of works, lest anyone should boast.
>
> —From the Letter of Paul to the Ephesians (Ephesians 2:8–9)

All Spiritual Types are common in Mainline Protestantism, including a large percentage of SCs.

Social activism is a common spiritual practice of Mainline Protestants. Feeding the hungry, sheltering the homeless, brokering peace between enemies, and other social and political causes are often pursued with spiritual vigor, following the words of Jesus in the Sermon on the Mount (Matthew 5–7): "Blessed are the merciful, for they will receive mercy…. Blessed are the peacemakers, for they will be called children of God."

A Mainline Protestant You Should Know:
John Shelby Spong (b. 1931)

In the last three decades, John Shelby Spong, recently retired bishop of the Episcopal Church's Newark, New Jersey, diocese, has become his church's preeminent social critic. The issues that have brought Spong the greatest notoriety have concerned sexuality. In the mid-1980s he commissioned a task force to study the increase in non-married young people living together, unmarried older people living together for economic reasons, and people in homosexual relationships. Spong and his task force concluded that sex inside of marriage was not always holy and can be abused, and that sex—homosexual or heterosexual—not blessed by marriage might also be holy. Convinced that gays should be fully included in the Church, Spong ordained an openly gay man in 1989, to the disdain of many of his colleagues. His books include *Living in Sin? A Bishop Rethinks Human Sexuality* (HarperSanFrancisco), *Rescuing the Bible from Fundamentalism* (HarperSanFrancisco), and his autobiography, *Here I Stand: My Struggle for a Christianity of Integrity, Love, and Equality* (HarperSanFrancisco).

Books

Borg, Marcus J. *The God We Never Knew: Beyond Dogmatic Religion to a More Authentic Contemporary Faith*. San Francisco: HarperSanFrancisco, 1998.

———. *The Heart of Christianity: Rediscovering a Life of Faith*. San Francisco: HarperSanFrancisco, 2003.

Buechner, Frederick. *The Alphabet of Grace*. San Francisco: HarperSanFrancisco, 1989.

Norris, Kathleen. *Dakota: A Spiritual Geography*. Boston: Houghton Mifflin, 1994.

Spong, John Shelby. *A New Christianity for a New World: Why Traditional Faith Is Dying and How a New Faith Is Being Born*. San Francisco: HarperSanFrancisco, 2001.

For More Information

Mainline Protestant churches are easily located across North America.

Ecunet: Faith Communities Online
Website: www.ecunet.org

Kirkridge
A Retreat and Study Center
2495 Fox Gap Rd.
Bangor, PA 18013-6028
Telephone: (610) 588-1793
Website: www.kirkridge.org

The National Council of Churches
475 Riverside Dr., Suite 880
New York, NY 10115
Telephone: (212) 870-2227
Website: www.ncccusa.org

> > Evangelical Christian Spirituality

Evangelical Christianity is the fastest-growing segment of American Protestantism, familiar to many through television. This Christian spirituality encompasses every Spiritual Type, but the Faithful Types predominate. Protestant denominations and groups such as Southern Baptists, the Church of the Nazarene, Pentecostals,* and Assemblies of God, as well as thousands of independent Christian churches, are strongly identified with Evangelical Christianity.

Evangelical Christians believe in the truth and infallibility of the Bible, and are unique among Christians in that they often use the Bible as direct evidence of God's will for all people. Perhaps most important to Evangelical Christians is the belief that salvation is found only in the acceptance of Jesus Christ as one's personal lord and savior, and in entering into an intimate relationship with him. This is the "born again" experience to which Evangelicals refer—a phrase that originates with the New Testament. Evangelicals further believe that God wants—

and even requires—them to spread the "good news" of salvation through Christ to everyone in the world. This belief is based on the words of Jesus in Matthew 28:19–20.

Evangelical worship services resemble those of other Protestant denominations, but are often more informal, lively, and emotional. At the end of

> Go therefore and make disciples of all nations, baptizing them in the name of the Father, and of the Son, and of the Holy Spirit, teaching them to observe all that I have commanded you; and lo, I am with you always, to the close of the age.
>
> —Jesus, in Matthew 27:19–20

each service, an invitation often is given for people to come forward and publicly acknowledge their need for salvation. Billy Graham, the well-known Evangelical Christian preacher, makes this kind of invitation at the conclusion of each of his services.

An Evangelical Christian You Should Know: Philip Yancey (b. 1940)

Philip Yancey is a journalist and popular author, a featured columnist for *Christianity Today*—one of the most widely read Evangelical Christian magazines in the world today. As a journalist, Yancey has interviewed people as diverse as President Bill Clinton and John Updike, but he is best known as an inspirational writer who explores ideas that are key to the Evangelical way of spirituality. His books include *Reaching for the Invisible God* (Zondervan) and *What's So Amazing About Grace?* (Zondervan). The "grace" he writes about is the freely given and unmerited favor and love of God, a grace which is viewed as the true message of Jesus Christ. Yancey calls "ungrace" a state of being in which self-righteousness and pride result in our thinking that we have somehow earned God's approval, and as a result are capable of standing in judgment on our own behalf.

Books

Graham, Billy. *Just As I Am: The Autobiography of Billy Graham*. San Francisco: HarperCollins, 1997.

Lucado, Max. *The Applause of Heaven*. Nashville, Tenn.: Word Books, 1999.

McDowell, Josh. *New Evidence That Demands a Verdict*. Nashville, Tenn.: Thomas Nelson, 1999.

Periodicals

Christianity Today
465 Gundersen Dr.
Carol Stream, IL 60188
Telephone: (630) 260-6200
Websites: www.christianity.net and www.christianityonline.com

For More Information

Evangelical churches are found across North America. Due to their Evangelical outlook, they are seldom hard to locate. Look for the word *Evangelical* in the church's name; or, if you are uncertain whether the church is Evangelical, simply call and ask the pastor.

Billy Graham Evangelistic Association
P.O. Box 1270
Charlotte, NC 28201
Telephone: (877) 247-2426
Website: www.billygraham.org

The National Association of Evangelicals
P.O. Box 23269
Washington, DC 20026
Telephone: (202) 789-1011
Website: www.nae.net

› › *Pentecostal Spirituality*

Pentecostal worship is emotional, energetic, and demonstrative. Most often united in belief with Evangelical Christians,* Pentecostal Christians also hold that a second baptism, a "Baptism of the Holy Spirit," is necessary to live a completely fulfilled spiritual life. This second baptism is no liturgical rite, but rather an outpouring of joy and exuberance that is given to the believer who prays for it. One of the results of the Baptism of the Holy Spirit is thought to be the gift of "speaking in tongues"—the sudden ability to speak in an unknown language that can be interpreted for the benefit of others by those with another of the gifts, the gift of prophecy. Pentecostals place great importance on miraculous healing as well, which often takes place within the context of their worship services. It is rare for a Skeptical Spiritual Type to find a home in Pentecostal Christianity.

> When the day of Pentecost had come, they were all gathered together in one place. And suddenly a sound came from heaven like the rush of a mighty wind, and it filled all the house where they were sitting. And there appeared to them tongues as of fire, distributed and resting on each one of them. And they were all filled with the Holy Spirit and began to speak in other tongues as the Spirit gave them utterance.
>
> —Acts 2:1–4

The Pentecostal movement began in Kansas around 1900, led by a former Methodist minister, C. F. Parham. Parham believed that an outpouring of the Holy Spirit, such as occurred shortly after Jesus' ascension as recorded in the New Testament's Book of Acts, would be a sign of the end of time, which he perceived to be imminent—as most Pentecostals do to this day. Other Evangelical Christian denominations are very similar to Pentecostal churches in holding this belief, including Holiness and Assembly of God churches—and there have even been occasional outpourings of

Pentecostal-style worship among Catholics* and Mainline Protestants* as well.

A Pentecostal You Should Know: Benny Hinn (b.1953)

Benny Hinn was born in Israel of an Armenian mother and Greek father, and was raised in the Greek Orthodox Church. At the age of eleven, he says, God appeared to him for the first time and has continued to appear to him in years since. At fourteen, he emigrated with his parents to Canada. In 1972, he experienced being "born again" at a revival led by the renowned evangelist Kathryn Kuhlman and began his preaching career very shortly thereafter, with little by way of formal training.

Hinn's services are characterized by miraculous healing. Many people at the services also experience being "slain in the spirit," falling to the floor uncontrollably when Hinn touches them. For many years Hinn was pastor of the ten-thousand-member Orlando Christian Center in Orlando, Florida. His television show, *This Is Your Day,* appears daily in many areas.

Books

Frost, Robert. *Aglow with the Spirit.* North Brunswick, N.J.: Bridge-Logos Publishers, 1992.
Hinn, Benny. *The Anointing.* Nashville, Tenn.: Thomas Nelson, 1997.
Synan, Vinson. *The Pentecostal-Holiness Tradition: Charismatic Movements in the Twentieth Century.* Grand Rapids, Mich.: W. B. Eerdmans Publishing Co., 1997.

For More Information

Pentecostal churches are usually easy to find across America. Look for the terms *Pentecostal, Holiness*, and *Assembly of God.*

86 • *Setting Out on Your Path*

General Council of the Assemblies of God
1445 Boonville Ave.
Springfield, MO 65802-1894
Telephone: (417) 862-2781
Website: www.ag.org

International Pentecostal Holiness Church
P.O. Box 12609
Oklahoma City, OK 73157
Telephone: (405) 787-7110
Website: www.iphc.org

United Pentecostal Churches International
Website: www.upci.org

> > Quaker Spirituality

Many SCs and FCs have found a home in this group more properly known as the Religious Society of Friends (the name "Quaker" was applied to the first members by observers who were amused by their habit of "quaking," or trembling, during worship). Quakers' main form of worship is contemplative—they gather in their meeting house (*not* called a "church") on Sundays and other times to sit in silence with each other for an unspecified period of time. There are no sermons, no hymns, no sacraments, no priests or ministers.

The Society of Friends was founded by the seventeenth-century English freethinking reformer George Fox. Fox sought to create a radically egalitarian, spirit-inspired Christianity that didn't rely on the intellectualism or the hierarchy of the Anglican Church of his time. Central to Quaker belief is that the saving knowledge and power of God, the "inner light," is present in all people. This conviction has had profound implications: it has resulted in the Quakers' near absence of centralized leadership, and in the creation of the unique Quaker form of governance by consensus. Quaker beliefs have also resulted throughout their history in the dedication to, and spiritual practice of, pacifism, nonviolence, and the struggle for equal rights for all.

A Quaker You Should Know: Richard J. Foster

Richard J. Foster's work celebrates the potential and strength of Christian spiritual disciplines to cultivate a deeper, more joyful inner life. Foster especially embraces the notions of simplicity, prayer, and solitude as ways to live in harmony with the rich complexity of life, and especially as antidotes to the hectic pace of the modern world. His books include *Prayer: Finding the Heart's True Home* (HarperSanFrancisco) and *Seeking the Kingdom: Devotions from the Daily Journey of Faith* (HarperSanFrancisco). Foster is a theology professor and also the executive director of the Milton Center for Excellence in Christian Writing. The center, which is located at Newman University in Wichita, Kansas, supports work by writers who seek to animate the Christian imagination, foster intellectual integrity, and explore the human condition with honesty and compassion.

> All Friends everywhere, this I charge you, which is the word of the Lord God unto you all, live in peace, in Christ, the way of peace, and therein seek the peace of all men, and no man's hurt. . . . It is love that overcomes and not hatred with hatred, nor strife with strife. Therefore live all in the peaceable life, doing good to all men.
>
> —George Fox, founder of the Religious Society of Friends

Books

Bacon, Margaret Hope. *The Quiet Rebels: The Story of the Quakers in America*. Wallingford, Pa.: Pendle Hill Publications, 2000.

Brinton, Howard, H.. *Friends for Three Hundred Years*. Wallingford, Pa.: Pendle Hill Publications, 1952.

Fox, George. *The Journal*. New York: Penguin USA, 1999.
Steere, Douglas, ed. *Quaker Spirituality*. Mahwah, N.J.: Paulist Press, 1984.

For More Information

Friends General Conference
1216 Arch St., 2B
Philadelphia, PA 19107
Telephone: (215) 561-1700
Website: www.fgcquaker.org

Friends United Meeting
101 Quaker Hill Dr.
Richmond, IN 47374-1980
Telephone: (765) 962-7573
Website: www.fum.org

Friends World Committee
1506 Race St.
Philadelphia, PA 19102
Telephone: (215) 241-7150
Website: www.fwccamericas.org

Pendle Hill: A Quaker Center for Study and Contemplation
338 Plush Mill Rd.
Wallingford, PA 19086
Telephone: (800) 742-3150
Website: www.pendlehill.org

› › Mennonite Spirituality

What separates Mennonites from most other Protestant* denominations is their church's stand on war and violence. Believing that Jesus taught the way to peace, Mennonites have always refused to participate in wars and have opposed capital punishment. They have also been vocal advocates for peace and reconciliation. Their nonviolent principle is central to Mennonite spirituality, based on the injunction of Jesus in the Gospels to "turn the other cheek" (Matthew 5:39). Other common Mennonite spiritual practices center around the belief that Christians are called by God to take on roles as humble servants of each other and the world; thus Mennonites advocate simple dress and simple lifestyle.

Mennonites are closely related to the Amish and Hutterites, as well as to the Church of the Brethren—all of these groups grew out of the Anabaptist movement of the Protestant Reformation (sixteenth century), whose members felt the early Protestant reformers were not sufficiently radical.

The nearly twenty groups of Mennonites in North America vary in lifestyle and religious practice. One feature they have in common is the way in which they differ with mainstream Protestants on when baptism should occur. Mennonites, and all Anabaptist groups, believe that Christians should be baptized after reaching an "age of accountability," usually early adolescence, when they are able to consciously choose their faith.

> As followers of Jesus, we participate in his ministry of peace and justice. He has called us to find our blessing in making peace and seeking justice. We do so in a spirit of gentleness, willing to be persecuted for righteousness' sake. As disciples of Christ, we do not prepare for war, or participate in war or military service. The same Spirit that empowered Jesus also empowers us to love enemies, to forgive rather than to seek revenge, to practice right relationships, to rely on the community of faith to settle disputes, and to resist evil without violence.
>
> —from the Confession of Faith of the General Conference Mennonite Church

A Mennonite You Should Know: Doris Longacre (1940–1979)

When Doris Longacre wrote *The More-with-Less Cookbook* (Herald Press), she was responding to what she called the "holy frustration" of fellow Mennonites. These worshipers wanted to comply with the

Mennonite Central Committee's request for each Mennonite household to decrease its total intake of food by as much as ten percent in order to "eat responsibly" and help reverse the world food crisis. *More-with-Less*, which has sold more than 650,000 copies to date, is more than a blueprint about how to cook healthy, nutritious, relatively inexpensive food. It also reflects Mennonite values: help the poor, the underprivileged, the hungry; be responsible for the environment. Longacre calls for a "Christ-sponsored sharing" to more equally distribute food: "As Christians dealing with human hurts, we have to remind ourselves that we are not called to be successful, but to be faithful. Our first directions come from the way Jesus told us to love, not from what we think will work."

Books

Dyck, Cornelius J. *An Introduction to Mennonite History: A Popular History of the Anabaptists and the Mennonites.* Scottdale, Pa.: Herald Press, 1993.

Good, Merle, and Phyllis Pellman Good. *Twenty Most-Asked Questions about the Amish and Mennonites.* Intercourse, Pa.: Good Books, 1995.

Horst, Isaac R. *A Separate People: An Insider's View of Old Order Mennonite Customs and Traditions.* Scottdale, Pa.: Herald Press, 2000.

Wenger, J. C. *What Mennonites Believe.* Scottdale, Pa.: Herald Press, 1991.

For More Information

Highland Retreat Center of the Mennonite Church
14783 Upper Highland Dr.
Bergton, VA 22811
Telephone: (540) 852-3226

Mennonite Central Committee
21 S. 12th St.
P.O. Box 500

Akron, PA 17501-0500
Telephone: (888) 563-4676
Website: www.mcc.org

Mennonite Church USA
500 S. Main St.
P.O. Box 1245
Elkhart, IN 46515-1245
Telephone: (574) 294-7523
Website: www.mennoniteusa.org

› Eastern Orthodox Spirituality

The Eastern Orthodox Church has seen a rise in the number of converts in recent decades, many of whom would likely be Spiritual Type FC—people seeking to combine faithfulness to traditional Christian teachings with an interest in mysticism. The Orthodox Church (often best known by its various ethnic designations such as Greek, Russian, Ukrainian, or Antiochian [Arabic] Orthodox) is distinguished by its rich and sensuous liturgy, which has changed little in 1,500 years. The celebration of the Eucharist, called the Divine Liturgy, is the central act of worship. Celebrated on Sunday and other Church holidays, the Divine Liturgy is entirely sung or chanted and takes approximately two hours to complete. Orthodox Christians have a highly developed theology of the image, and their churches are filled

> **The Lenten Prayer of St. Ephrem of Syria**
>
> O Lord and master of my life,
> Take from me the spirit of sloth,
> despair, lust of power, and idle talk;
> But grant rather the spirit of chastity, humility, patience, and love to your servant.
> Yes, O Lord and King, grant me to see my own faults, and not to judge my brother and sister, for you are blessed unto ages of ages. Amen.

with icons, or holy pictures, used in worship and personal devotion.

The Orthodox celebrate the same sacraments as do Roman Catholics,* and share their devotion to the saints and the Virgin Mary. The practice of fasting is more prevalent in Orthodoxy than in any other Christian body—with abstinence from animal products encouraged on every Wednesday and Friday and during four different Lenten periods each year. Monasticism has been of great importance, with monks and nuns among the most influential spiritual teachers.

Orthodoxy is especially known for a method of prayer called *hesychasm*, which has been influential in every traditionally Orthodox country. In imitation of the admonition of St. Paul to "pray without ceasing" (1 Thessalonians 5:17) the *hesychast* repeats a simple prayer. This prayer is usually "Lord Jesus Christ, have mercy upon me," and they repeat it continuously, with the mouth, then with the mind, and finally—literally—with the heart, until he or she is completely absorbed by the prayer and it becomes as natural as a heartbeat.

Associated primarily with Greece, Russia, Eastern Europe, and the Middle East, the Eastern Orthodox Church became separated from the Western Roman Catholic Church over a period of several centuries around the turn of the first millennium, over differences that were political as well as theological. The Orthodox have no central figure of authority comparable to the Catholic pope. There is instead usually a presiding bishop of each country, called a patriarch or metropolitan.

An Eastern Orthodox Christian You Should Know: Starets Silouan of Mount Athos (1866–1938)

Starets ("elder" in Russian) Silouan was a peasant from the Tambov region of Russia, who, at the age of twenty, decided to become a monk. Rather than settling in one of the monastic communities of his native land, he traveled to the Monastery of St. Panteleimon—the main Russian monastery on Mount Athos, the pan-Orthodox monastic republic in present-day Greece—where he remained the rest of his life. Starets Silouan was a practitioner of *hesychasm*, an ancient art of prayer that is the foundation of Eastern Orthodox spirituality. The joy of his presence made an impact on everyone who ever met him—to the extent that, in spite of his obscure situation, he became an inspiration and example for Orthodox Christians throughout the world and remains so to this day. Father Silouan is an example of a great *hesychast* who lived in the twentieth century. Two books have been written about his life and teaching, both by Archimandrite Sophrony: *The Monk of Mount Athos* (SVS Press) and *Wisdom from Mount Athos* (SVS Press).

Books

Pennington, M. Basil. *The Monks of Mount Athos: A Western Monk's Extraordinary Spiritual Journey on Eastern Holy Ground.* Woodstock, Vt.: SkyLight Paths, 2003.

Schmemann, Alexander. *For the Life of the World: Sacraments and Orthodoxy.* Crestwood, N.Y.: St. Vladimir's Seminary Press, 1997.

Ware, Kallistos T. *The Orthodox Way.* Crestwood, N.Y.: St. Vladimir's Seminary Press, 1995.

Ware, Timothy. *The Orthodox Church.* New York: Penguin USA, 1993.

The Way of a Pilgrim: Annotated and Explained. Translated and annotated by Gleb Pokrovsky. Woodstock, Vt.: SkyLight Paths, 2001.

For More Information

Eastern Orthodox Churches are often listed in the phone book under "Eastern Orthodox," "Greek Orthodox," "Russian Orthodox," "Ukrainian Orthodox," "Romanian Orthodox," or "Orthodox Church in America." If you are unable to locate a parish in your area, contact:

The Antiochian Orthodox Christian Archdiocese of North America
358 Mountain Rd.

P.O. Box 5238
Englewood, NJ 07631-5238
Telephone: (201) 871-1355
Website: www.antiochian.org

The Greek Orthodox Archdiocese of North and South America
8 E. 79th St.
New York, NY 10021
Telephone: (212) 570-3500
Website: www.goarch.org

The Orthodox Church in America
6850 Hempstead Turnpike
P.O. Box 675
Syosset, NY 11791
Telephone: (516) 922-0550
Website: www.oca.org

Islamic Spirituality

The Arabic word *Islam* means "surrender," and Islam is a spirituality of surrender to God. Its beautiful simplicity is most often appealing to the two Faithful Types (FRs and FCs).

A follower of Islam is called a Muslim. One becomes a Muslim by making the declaration called the *shahada*: "There is no God but God; Muhammad is the messenger of God." (The name *Allah*, so much associated with Islam, is the Arabic word for God, used by Arabic-speaking Christians as well as Muslims). The *shahada* is one of the Five Pillars of Islam, five requirements of every Muslim. The other four are:

> Prayer five times daily, facing the direction of the holy city of Mecca, Saudi Arabia

> Sharing one's material wealth, especially with the poor and needy

> Fasting from food between sunrise and sunset every day during the month of Ramadan

> Pilgrimage to the holy city of Mecca at least once in one's life, unless prohibited by health or financial resources

Though its adherents regard it as the true religion that has always existed, Islam originated in the early seventh century in what is now Saudi Arabia. The prophet Muhammad was a merchant of the city of Mecca who suddenly and unexpectedly began to experience a series of overwhelming revelations from God. The revelations were recorded as the Qur'an (sometimes also spelled "Koran"), Islam's holy book, which is believed to contain the exact words given by God to Muhammad. Though his fellow Arabs were at first hostile toward the new monotheistic religion that Muhammad preached, by the time of the Prophet's death in 632 CE the entire Arabian peninsula had become Muslim. Within a very short time Islam extended from Africa to China and to the outskirts of Europe. Today Muslims are found in every country of the world, totaling nearly a billion.

A Muslim You Should Know: Seyyed Hossein Nasr (b. 1933)

Seyyed Hossein Nasr is the foremost scholar of Islam in the Western world; he is also one of Islam's most eloquent interpreters for Westerners. He was born in Iran and studied there as well as at Harvard University. From 1958 to 1979 he was a professor of philosophy at Teheran University, leaving at the time of that country's Islamic revolution to teach in the West. He is currently the University Professor of Islamic Studies at George Washington University in Washington, D.C., and the author of more than twenty books, which include *Knowledge and the Sacred* (SUNY Press) and *Man and Nature: The Spiritual Crisis of Modern Man* (Kazi Publications), in which he argues that the world environmental crisis is the result of mankind's loss of the religious understanding of nature.

> One day the Prophet was sitting with some people when the archangel Gabriel came to him and said, "What is faith?"
>
> The Prophet replied, "Faith is to believe in God, in God's angels, and in meeting God; and in the messengers of God; and in the Resurrection."
>
> Gabriel said, "What is submission?"
>
> The Prophet replied, "Submission is to serve God and not attribute any partners to God, and to pray regularly, and to pay the prescribed welfare tax, and to fast during the month of Ramadan."
>
> Gabriel said, "What is goodness?"
>
> The prophet replied, "To worship God as if you actually see God; for if you do not see God, God certainly sees you."
>
> —from the *Hadith*, the sayings of the Prophet Muhammad

Books

Armstrong, Karen. *Islam: A Short History.* New York: Modern Library, 2002.

Chittick, William C. *Faith and Practice in Islam: Three Thirteenth-Century Sufi Texts.* Albany, N.Y.: SUNY Press, 1992.

Esposito, John L. *The Oxford History of Islam.* Oxford: Oxford Univ. Press, 1999.

Nasr, Seyyed Hossein. *The Heart of Islam: Enduring Values for Humanity.* San Francisco: HarperSanFrancisco, 2002.

Schimmel, Annemarie. *Islam: An Introduction.* Albany, N.Y.: SUNY Press, 1992.

Sells, Michael. *Approaching the Qur'an: The Early Revelations.* Ashland, Ore.: White Cloud Press, 2000.

For More Information

To find a mosque in America, consult Islamic Finder, at the website: www.islamicfinder.org. Other resources are:

Islamic Assembly of North America
3588 Plymouth Rd., Suite 270
Ann Arbor, MI 48105
Telephone: (734) 528-0006
Website: www.iananet.org

Islamic Circle of North America
166-26 89th Ave.
Jamaica, NY 11432
Telephone: (718) 658-1199
Website: www.icna.org

Islamic Society of North America
P.O. Box 38
Plainfield, IN 46168
Telephone: (317) 839-8157
Website: www.isna.net

› Sufi Spirituality

Sufism is a mystical movement within Islam, appealing most often to the two Contemplative Spiritual Types, FC and SC. The Sufi way is a path of purification, a discipline of mind and body whose goal is to experience the ultimate reality directly. Sufis speak of burning away the *nafs*, the lower self, to reveal the higher self that is inherently one with God. Some of the practices engaged in to attain this are meditation, *dhikr*—the rhythmic repetition of one of the names of God, done either by individuals or by groups—and the famous turning dance of the Mevlevi, "whirling dervishes."

The Sufis have no central organization but are organized into numerous interrelated communities—called schools, lodges, or orders—several of which are active in North America. The practices of each community vary widely, but all of them have at heart the fervent desire for the close, direct, and personal experience of God.

The origins of Sufism are obscure, but some Muslims claim that Sufism is actually the truest form of Islam and that the prophet Muhammad and his Companions were the first Sufis.

> **Desolation**
> For the servant of God
> Consolation is the place of danger
> Where he may be deluded
> (Accepting only what he sees,
> Experiences, knows)
> But desolation is his home:
> For in desolation he is seized by
>   God
> And entirely taken over into God.
> In darkness, in emptiness
> In loss, in death of self.
> Then the self is only ashes. Not
>   even ashes!
>
> —Ibn Abbad (fourteenth century)

Sufi groups have arisen wherever Islam has been prevalent, from Africa to parts of China. In recent years, Sufism has become more familiar to people of all faiths and backgrounds through the popularity of the poetry of Rumi, a twelfth-century Sufi mystic who is currently the best-selling poet in North America.

A Sufi You Should Know: Bawa Muhaiyadeen (d. 1986)

Muhammad Raheem Bawa Muhaiyaddeen was one of the first modern Sufi masters to teach in North America. Little is known of his early personal history. Records of his life began in the early 1900s when religious pilgrims traveling through the jungles of Sri Lanka first caught a glimpse of him. He became a beloved figure in the predominantly Buddhist Sri Lanka, consulted by people of all religions. In 1971 he accepted an invitation to visit the United States, where he ended up settling in Philadelphia, continuing to teach and give discourses right up until his death. His charismatic presence drew people of all faiths to him—as had happened also in Sri Lanka. Wherever he went, he tirelessly answered the many personal and mystical questions that people brought. His discourses and sayings have been collected into a number of books, including, *To Die Before Death: A Sufi Way of Life* and *The Wisdom of Man* (both Fellowship Press).

Books

Ernst, Carl W. *The Shambhala Guide to Sufism.* Boston: Shambhala Pubications, 1997.

Helminski, Kabir Edmund. *Living Presence: A Sufi Way to Mindfulness and the Essential Self.* New York: J. P. Tarcher, 1992.

Khan, Hazrat Inayat. *The Heart of Sufism: Essential Writings of Hazrat Inayat Khan.* Boston: Shambhala Publications, 1999.

Rumi, Jalaluddin. *Rumi and Islam: Selections from His Stories, Poems, and Discourses: Annotated and Explained.* Translated and annotated by Ibrahim Gamard. Woodstock, Vt.: SkyLight Paths, 2004.

Schimmel, Annemarie. *Mystical Dimensions of Islam.* Chapel Hill, N.C.: Univ. of North Carolina Press, 1985.

For More Information

There are a number of Sufi orders active in the United States. One of the organizations below should be able to put you in touch with one near you.

Bawa Muhaiyadeen Fellowship
5820 Overbrook Ave.
Philadelphia, PA 19131-1221
Telephone: (215) 879-6300
Website: www.bmf.org

Nimatullahi Sufi Order
306 W. 11th St.
New York, NY 10014
Telephone: (212) 924-7739
Website: www.nimatullahi.org

Sufi Order International
North American Secretariat
5 Abode Rd.
New Lebanon, NY 12125
Telephone: (518) 794-7834

Threshold Society
151 Emerald City Way
Watsonville, CA 95076
Telephone: (831) 685-3995
Website: www.sufism.org

› Bahá'í Spirituality

Bahá'ís believe in the unity of all humanity and of all religions, and that the time has come to manifest global unity. Their faith is particularly appealing to the Faithful Spiritual Types. Bahá'ís are enjoined to pray and meditate daily—though the form of meditation is not specified—and to read from the voluminous writings of their prophet, Bahá'u'lláh. Because of their concern with global unity, they are also often involved in peace and justice work, which they also regard as spiritual practice. Bahá'ís fast from food between sunrise and sunset every year for nineteen days in March, much as Muslims fast during the month of Ramadan.

The Bahá'í faith arose out of an Islamic movement called Babiism, which was founded in nineteenth-century Persia (now southern Iran) by Mirza Ali Muhammad, a direct descendant of the prophet Muhammad. Proclaiming himself the "Bab" (literally, "gate"), Ali Muhammad announced that he was the forerunner of God's universal messenger, who would soon arrive to inaugurate an era of justice and peace. The Bab was executed by firing squad in 1850. In 1863, Bahá'u'lláh, who had been one of the Bab's closest disciples, declared himself to be the

> I have awakened in Thy shelter, O my God, and it becometh him that seeketh that shelter to abide within the sanctuary of Thy protection and the Stronghold of Thy defense. Illumine my inner being, O my Lord, with the splendors of the Day-Spring of Thy Revelation, even as Thou didst illumine my outer being with the morning light of Thy favor.
>
> —Bahá'í Morning Prayer

one about whom the Bab had prophesied. Bahá'u'lláh taught that there have been a succession of prophets sent by God, each with a divine message that was appropriate for the era in which it appeared. Bahá'ís believe that Bahá'u'lláh is the prophet of our age, and that he will not be the last.

A Bahá'í You Should Know: Abdu'l Bahá (1844–1921)

Born Abbas Effendi, Bahá'u'lláh's oldest son took the new name Abdu'l Bahá ("servant of the glory") when he assumed leadership of the Bahá'í faith after his father's death in 1892. He spent the final years of the nineteenth century in Ottoman prisons, persecuted for his faith. After his release in 1908, he began a series of journeys in Europe and America that made the Bahá'í faith familiar to people far beyond his native Persia. Speaking in churches, schools, universities, and peace organizations, he left an indelible impression on every hearer, and ensured the propagation of the Bahá'í faith throughout the world more than any other person. An informative book that collects his spiritual teachings is *Wisdom of the Master,* edited by Steven Scholl (White Cloud Press).

Books

Bahá'u'lláh. *The Divine Art of Living: Selections from the Writings of Bahá'u'lláh and Abdu'l Bahá.* Wilmette, Ill.: Bahá'í Publishing Trust, 1985.

Effendi, Shoghi. *Epistle to the Son of the Wolf.* Wilmette, Ill.: Bahá'í Publishing Trust, 1985.

Esselmont, J.E. *Bahá'u'lláh and the New Era.* Wilmette, Ill.: Bahá'í Publishing Trust, 1980.

Periodical

One Country
The Online Newsletter of the Bahá'í International Community
Website: www.onecountry.org

For More Information

The following organization can put you in touch with a Bahá'í community in your area.

National Spiritual Assembly of the Bahá'ís of the United States
1233 Central St.
Evanston, IL 60201
Telephone: (800) 228-6483
Website: www.bahai.org

7 >

New Movements, Rediscovered Traditions, and Other Spiritualities

New Consciousness Spirituality

New Consciousness is not an organized religious or spiritual tradition, but rather, the term used by many people today who share the idea that the world is on the verge of (or may already have entered) a new era in which a higher level of consciousness than was previously possible is now attainable. (New Consciousness is a term that, for many, replaces the older term "New Age" in describing this movement; however, New Age is still prevalent as well.)

Recent studies have suggested that about one-sixth of all Americans agree with New Consciousness principles. Contemplative Spiritual Types are often quite at home in New Consciousness spirituality, which includes the belief that neither Eastern nor Western thought is the source of all knowledge. From the West has come democracy, equality, and modern physics, psychology and medicine; from the East have come interior disciplines for exploring the far reaches of consciousness and awareness.

New Consciousness spiritual practices are eclectic and range widely according to the individual, but may include: belief in astrology and reincarnation; divination methods such as Tarot; and "channelling," through which God or various entities speak through a chosen person. New Consciousness enthusiasts also often embrace select elements of other spiritual traditions such as Hinduism,* Gnosticism, Neopaganism, and Theosophy—usually reinterpreting them for modern purposes.

> The deepest secret is that life is not a process of discovery, but a process of creation. You are not discovering yourself, but creating yourself anew. Seek, therefore, not to find out Who You Are; seek to determine Who You Want to Be.
>
> —Neale Donald Walsch,
> *Conversations with God*

The net of the New Consciousness movement is very wide, encompassing all Spiritual Types and people from all backgrounds. Many people, for instance, remain within conventional religious traditions, adding New Consciousness beliefs and practices to their spirituality. Others, like the popular author Ken Wilber, lead the movement in some of its core beliefs, while disagreeing with many of its practices.

A New Consciousness Person You Should Know: Neale Donald Walsch (b. 1943)

In 1992, Neale Donald Walsch was a forty-nine-year-old newspaper editor living in Ashland, Oregon, stuck in a career that was no longer rewarding and in a relationship that was on the verge of breaking up. Early one morning, at a particularly difficult time in the crisis, he sat down and dashed off an angry letter to God as a way of "venting" his frustration with his situation. Just as he finished pouring out his soul in a series of angry questions, he was surprised that God began to answer his questions—in a strong and unmistakable inner voice that he was compelled to write down. The communications continued for years, and were eventually compiled into the phenomenally popular books *Conversations with God*, Books 1, 2, and 3 (see below for publisher information).

Books

Myss, Caroline. *Anatomy of the Spirit: The Seven Stages of Power and Healing*. New York: Random House, 1997.

Redfield, James. *The Celestine Prophecy: An Adventure*. New York: Warner Books, 1994.

Walsch, Neale Donald. *Bringers of the Light*. Charlottesville, Va.: Hampton Roads Publishing, 2000.

———. *Conversations with God: An Uncommon Dialogue, Book 1*: New York: Putnam, 1996. *Books 2 and 3*: Charlottesville, Va.: Hampton Roads Publishing, 1997.

———. *No Boundary: Eastern and Western Approaches to Psychological Growth*. New York: Random House, 1981.

———. *Sex, Ecology, Spirituality: The Spirit of Evolution*. Boston: Shambhala Publications, 1995.

———. *The Marriage of Sense and Soul: Integrating Science and Religion*. New York: Random House, 1998.

Wilber, Ken. *A Brief History of Everything*. Boston: Shambhala Publications, 1996.

Periodicals

Body and Soul Magazine
Whole Living
P.O. Box 2073
Marion, OH 43306-8173
Telephone: (800) 755-1178
Website: www.bodyandsoulmag.com

Magical Blend
133½ Broadway
Chico, CA 95928

Telephone: (530) 893-9037
Website: www.magicalblend.com

What Is Enlightenment?
Moksha Press
P.O. Box 2360
Lenox, MA 01240
Telephone: (800) 376-3210
Website: www.wie.org

For More Information

The New Consciousness movement is not centrally organized—there are no New Consciousness organizations as such. Some of the best sources for more information are the periodicals listed above.

› Celtic Spirituality

Both FCs and SCs may find themselves drawn more than the other Spiritual Types into the Celtic tradition of mysticism through reverence for nature. The Celts became Christianized relatively early compared to the rest of Europe, and their church developed its own lively style and administration for several hundred years before it came under the influence of the Roman Catholic Church.* This spirit was never completely extinguished, adding several unique features to Christianity in Ireland, Scotland, Wales, Northumbria, and other places the Celts inhabited. These traditions are being rediscovered today, both by Christians and those from other spiritual traditions.

Celtic Spirituality is characterized by a deep reverence for nature, based on the view that human beings are part of the environment rather than a ruling force intended to dominate it. Other Celtic spiritual practices stem from envisioning the spiritual life as pilgrimage—a sort of eternal wandering toward God that never really ends. This notion of pilgrimage can be taken symbolically, or very literally—as it was by some members of the early Celtic Church who used long voyages as spiritual discipline, the famous St. Brendan among them.

Celtic tradition holds that there is a place where each of us will die and meet God face to face—that God has prepared that special place for each of us. It is there that we enter the kingdom of heaven. Many previously uninhabited islands in the Irish Sea were explored as

> Deep peace of the flowing streams to you
> Deep peace of the gentle breeze to you
> Deep peace of the dark earth to you
> Deep peace of the glittering stars to you
> Deep peace of the Lord Jesus to you.
>
> —A Celtic Blessing

Celts—and others since them—have wandered there with ideas like this in mind, following the words of Jesus from the Gospel of John: "In my father's house there are many mansions.... I go to prepare a place for you" (John 14:2).

A Celtic Spiritual Writer You Should Know: John O'Donohue (b. 1956)

An Irish poet, scholar, and expert on Celtic mythology and spirituality, John O'Donohue has made the connection between traditional Christianity and the Celtic celebration of bodily wisdom. He argues that since the Celts were not subjected to persecutions the way Christians were in continental Europe, they were better able to wed pagan sensuality with the ethical imperatives of the Christian faith. He has written that the Western world has been "dominated by thinking that there's only one self inside of us. That's far too simple. There are many different selves inside every individual." In his book *Anam Cara* (HarperCollins), O'Donohue explores these secret universes we all carry inside us, the connections we forge with the worlds of our friends and loved ones, and the products of our worlds reflected in the things we create outside of ourselves. He teaches that the comprehension of the sublime architecture of the worlds we are born with engenders a new appreciation for the outside world and the way we care for it, and contributes to its evolution.

Books

Cowan, Tom. *Yearning for the Wind: Celtic Reflections on Nature and the Soul.* Novato, Calif.: New World Library, 2003.
Cronin, Deborah K. *Holy Ground: Celtic Christian Spirituality.* Nashville, Tenn.: Upper Room, 1999.
Davies, Oliver, and Thomas O'Loughlin, eds. *Celtic Spirituality (Classics of Western Spirituality Series).* New York: Paulist Press, 1999.
De Waal, Esther. *The Celtic Way of Prayer.* New York: Doubleday, 1997.
Freeman, Mara. *Kindling the Celtic Spirit: Ancient Traditions to Illumine Your Life Throughout the Seasons.* San Francisco: HarperSanFrancisco, 2001.
Joyce, Timothy J. *Celtic Christianity: A Sacred Tradition, a Vision of Hope.* Maryknoll, N.Y.: Orbis Books, 1998.
Newell, Philip J. *Listening for the Heartbeat of God: A Celtic Spirituality.* Mahwah, N.J.: Paulist Press, 1998.

For More Information

Advocates of Celtic Spirituality often worship within the Roman Catholic* tradition, but Celtic Spirituality is also broadly ecumenical. One active Celtic group today is the Iona Community, located on a small island off the west coast of Scotland, where St. Columba founded a Celtic monastery in the sixth century CE. People of all faiths are welcome there for retreats and other educational events. Other independent Celtic groups are also listed below.

Celtic Christian Church
P.O. Box 299

Canadensis, PA 18325-0299
Telephone: (570) 595-2543

The Iona Community
4th Floor, Savoy House
140 Sauchiehall St.
Glasgow G2 3DH
Scotland
Telephone: 0141 332-6343
Website: www.iona.org.uk

St. Brendan's Abbey of the Culdees
120 N. Fifth St.
Springfield, OR 97477
Telelphone: (541) 741-2693

› Creation Spirituality

Advocates of Creation Spirituality are found among all Spiritual Types, but most commonly among the Skeptical-Contemplative Type, or SC. Though its origins are Christian,* Creation Spirituality proponents assert that its ideals transcend religious boundaries, and that it is in fact the essence of all true religion, being found in each of them in a distinctive flavor. Thus its followers partake in a range of spiritual practices taken from many traditions.

The basis of Creation Spirituality is found in the following ten principles:

1 › The universe is basically a blessing, that is, something we experience as good.

2 › Everyone is a mystic—born full of wonder and capable of recovering it at any age.

3 › Everyone is a prophet, a mystic in action, who is called to interfere with anything that interrupts authentic life.

4› Humans have to dig and work at finding their true self.

5› Salvation is best understood as "preserving the good."

6› The journey that marks that digging can be named as a fourfold journey: (1) *via positiva*: delight, awe, wonder, revelry; (2) *via negativa*: darkness, silence, suffering, letting go; (3) *via creativa*: birthing, creativity; and (4) *via transformativa*: compassion, justice healing, celebration.

7› Everyone is an artist in some way, and art as meditation is a primary form of prayer.

8› We are all sons and daughters of God; therefore, we have divine blood in our veins, the divine breath in our lungs; and the basic work of God is: Compassion.

9› Divinity is as much Mother as Father, as much Child as Parent, as much Godhead (mystery) as God (history), as much beyond all beings as in all beings.

10› We experience the Divine in all things and all things are in the Divine.

Antiphon for the Creator

Oh, how wonderful is
the prescience of the divine Heart
who foreknew all Creation.
For looking on the face of Man
  new-formed,
He saw completed in this form—
  Creation.
Oh, how wonderful is the breath
that breathed Man to life.

—Hildegard of Bingen (1098–1179)

An Advocate of Creation Spirituality You Should Know: Matthew Fox (b. 1940)

Father Matthew Fox may not take credit for founding Creation Spirituality, but he can be credited with coining the term. He began writing about Creation Spirituality in the 1980s, while still a Catholic priest of the Dominican order. His theological views were controversial enough to get him expelled from the order, and he was later also silenced by the Vatican for a year before finally being removed from the priesthood altogether (he was then received into the Episcopal Church as a priest). He is the founder and president of the University of Creation Spirituality in Oakland, California. Fox is the author of more than twenty books, including *A Spirituality Named Compassion* (Inner Traditions); *Breakthrough: Meister Eckhart's Creation Spirituality in New Translation;* and (with scientist Rupert Sheldrake) *Natural Grace: Dialogues on Creation, Darkness, and Soul in Spirituality* (Main Street Books). He is also, in large part, responsible for the contemporary resurgence of interest in the medieval visionary Hildegard of Bingen.

Books

Fox, Matthew. *The Coming of the Cosmic Christ: The Healing of Mother Earth and the Birth of a Global Renaissance.* San Francisco: HarperSanFrancisco, 1988.

———. *Creation Spirituality: Liberating Gifts for the Peoples of the Earth.* San Francisco: HarperSanFrancisco, 1991.

———. *Creativity: Where the Divine and the Human Meet.* New York: Jeremy P. Tarcher/Putnam, 2002.

———. *Original Blessing: A Primer on Creation Spirituality.* Santa Fe, N. M.: Bear & Co., Inc., 1996.

For More Information

University of Creation Spirituality
2141 Broadway
Oakland, CA 94612-2309
Telephone: (510) 835-4827
Website: www.creationspirituality.com

› Unity Spirituality

The Unity movement blends Christian concepts with broader New Consciousness* concerns, and appeals strongly to both the Faithful and Contemplative Spiritual Types (FC, FR, and SC). Favoring a fervently positive approach to life, Unity teaching holds that God has many attributes, the most important of which is love. The affirmation statement of the Unity movement is this: "I daily dedicate myself to demonstrate the unconditional love and faith in Jesus Christ."

> The same spirit that lives in Jesus Christ lives in each one of us, making God's power and love available to us always.
>
> —from Unity's Six Basic Truths

Founded by Charles and Myrtle Fillmore in the late nineteenth century, the Unity movement stresses that God's divinity is not limited, but that God is Spirit and is present everywhere and in everyone. Unity denies the existence of any power or presence opposed to God. It acknowledges that evil and suffering appear in the world, but ascribes these to humanity's ignorance and misuse of God's laws of life. While proclaiming the divinity of Jesus, Unity goes further by proclaiming that all of us are divine in nature, and that Jesus expressed his divine potential to show the rest of us how to express ours as well. These beliefs are foundational to spiritual practice in the Unity tradition, which focuses on personal prayer, cultivating a spiritual imagination, and focusing on the abundant goodness of life with God as the ultimate source of all. Unity holds that the mind is our connecting link to God, that there is good in every religion, and that the present moment is part of our eternal life.

A Unity Spiritual Leader You Should Know: Marianne Williamson (b. 1952)

Marianne Williamson is an internationally acclaimed author and lecturer. Formerly the spiritual leader of the four-thousand-member Unity Church of Today in the Detroit suburb of Warren, she continues to draw large crowds for her spiritual teaching in the church's reorganization as the Renaissance Unity Church. She is the author of several best-selling books and a frequent lecturer to large audiences around the country. She first caught wide public attention in the late 1980s with her book, *A Return to Love: Reflections on the Principles of a Course in Miracles* (HarperCollins). (*A Course in Miracles* by Helen Schucman was first published in the mid-1970s and became a bestseller. A self-study course in spiritual psychology, it focuses on the Christian principles of universal love and forgiveness.) In *A Return to Love*, Williamson teaches how we can all become miracle workers by accepting God and by expressing love in our daily lives. Williamson has since written several other books, including *The Healing of America* (Simon & Schuster). She is a cofounder of the Global Renaissance Alliance, which promotes nonviolence and the introduction of spiritual values into the political system.

Books

Fillmore, Charles. *The Essential Charles Fillmore: Collected Writings of a Missouri Mystic*. Unity Village, Mo.: Unity School of Christianity, 1999.

Rosemergy, Jim. *The Quest for Meaning: Living a Life of Purpose*. Unity Village, Mo.: Unity School of Christianity, 1998.

Williamson, Marianne. *A Return to Love: Reflections on the Principles of a Course in Miracles*. New York: HarperCollins, 1996.

———. *Everyday Grace: Having Hope, Finding Forgiveness, and Making Miracles*. New York: Riverhead Books, 2002.

Periodical

Unity Magazine
A Spiritual Resource for Daily Living
1901 N.W. Blue Parkway
Unity Village, MO 64065-0001
Telephone: (816) 524-3550
Website: www.unityonline.org

For More Information

The Association of Unity Churches
P.O. Box 610
Lee's Summit, MO 64063
Website: www.unity.org

Unity School of Christianity
1901 N.W. Blue Parkway
Unity Village, MO 64065-0001
Telephone: (816) 524-3550

› Wiccan Spirituality

Wicca is a contemporary rediscovery of the ancient, pre-Christian spiritual tradition of Europe. Most Wiccans maintain what is referred to as a panentheistic view of the cosmos—that the Divine is *in* everything around us—which leads to their great reverence for the earth.

The modern Wicca movement is organized around spiritual practices that generally fall into one of three categories: (1) "old religion" Wicca, which follows the seasonal cycles of nature, focusing on festival celebrations of the solstices and equinoxes, sometimes on the midpoints between them, and of the new and full moons; (2) polytheistic Wicca, with worship of multiple local goddesses and gods; and, (3) simple *magick* practice (spelled with a *k* to distinguish it from non-spiritual magic).

> An ye harm none, do what ye will.
>
> —The Wiccan Rede

Wiccan gatherings are called covens, but it is also common for Wiccans to practice alone, particularly those who focus on *magick*, whose practice is sometimes called "eclectic" practice.

Some Wiccans call themselves witches, and they practice witchcraft, but they battle the "Halloween" stereotype associated with those terms. Wicca is sometimes also simply called "the craft." Witches use spells as an important part of their practice, but for the purpose of channeling the divine energy we all naturally possess—not for evil purposes, as is sometimes thought. Another common misconception about Wiccans is that they are Satanists. This is untrue—Satan is a Christian concept, and the pagan Wiccan tradition predates Christianity,* probably by millennia. Wicca has seen rapid growth in recent decades, particularly among Skeptical Spiritual Types, and those seeking woman-positive, earth-based religion.

A Wiccan You Should Know: Laurie Cabot

Laurie Cabot has been a practitioner of witchcraft for more than forty years. She is founder of the Cabot Tradition of the Science of Witchcraft and the Witches' League for Public Awareness (WLPA), an anti-defamation group aimed at correcting misconceptions about witchcraft. Through lectures at colleges and universities and her appearances on National Public Radio and on such television shows as *The Oprah Winfrey Show* and *Unsolved Mysteries,* she has helped educate the public about witchcraft, which she and other Wiccans consider to be the oldest nature religion.

Cabot lives in Salem, Massachusetts, where she teaches classes on a number of Wiccan topics. Her books, including *The Witch in Every Woman* (Delta Books), have been published in the United States, Australia, Britain, Denmark, Japan, and Russia.

Books

Adler, Margot. *Drawing Down the Moon: Witches, Druids, Goddess Worshippers, and Other Pagans in America Today*. New York: Penguin, 1997.
Cunningham, Scott. *Wicca: A Guide for the Solitary Practitioner*. St. Paul, Minn.: Llewellyn Publications, 1990.
Farrar, Janet, and Stewart Farrar. *A Witches' Bible: The Complete

Witches' Handbook. Blaine, Wash.: Phoenix Publishing, 1996.

Ravenwolf, Silver. *To Light a Sacred Flame: Practical Witchcraft for the Millennium.* St. Paul, Minn.: Llewellyn Publications, 1999.

Starhawk. *The Spiral Dance: A Rebirth of the Ancient Religion of the Great Goddess.* 20th Anniversary Ed. San Francisco: HarperSanFrancisco, 1999.

Periodical

Covenant of the Goddess
P.O. Box 1226
Berkeley, CA 94701
Website: www.cog.org

Reclaiming
P.O. Box 14404
San Francisco, CA 94114
Website: www.reclaiming.org

Sagewoman Magazine
P.O. Box 641
Point Arena, CA 95468
Telephone: (707) 882-2052
Website: www.sagewoman.com

For More Information

Wiccans are organized in covens across America. The following organizations may be able to help you locate one.

Witches' League for Public Awareness
P.O. Box 909
Rehoboth, MA 02769
Website: www.celticcrow.com

The Witches' Voice, Inc.
P.O. Box 4924
Clearwater, FL 33758-4924
Website: www.witchvox.com

Humanist Spirituality

People don't often speak of Humanism as a spirituality, since Humanists usually reject religion in all its forms, but as Skeptical-Rational (SR) Spiritual Types know, many things associated with spirituality—such as morality and insight—are not limited to religion. And Humanist spirituality is about much more than the rejection of organized religion.

Neither an organized movement or spiritual tradition, Humanist spirituality is nevertheless practiced by many people in both subtle and active ways. Humanists usually believe that each of us alone is responsible for any meaning our lives have or don't have. Humanists emphasize reason and scientific inquiry, individual freedom and responsibility, human values and compassion, and the need for tolerance and cooperation. They reject supernatural claims and all kinds of authoritarian beliefs and doctrines.

> I believe that when I die I shall rot, and nothing of my ego will survive. I am not young, and I love life. But I should scorn to shiver with terror at the thought of annihilation. Happiness is nonetheless true happiness because it must come to an end, nor do thought and love lose their value because they are not everlasting.
>
> —Bertrand Russell, from
> *Why I Am Not a Christian*

The spiritual practices of Humanists range widely, expressed in all of the diverse ways that people seek to improve themselves and the world. They recognize that values—whether religious, ethical, social, or political—have their source in human experience and effort. Humanists assert that humanity must take responsibility for its own destiny, a belief that perhaps informs the everyday actions of people of Humanist spirituality more than any other.

A Humanist You Should Know: Bertrand Russell (1872–1970)

Lord Bertrand Arthur William Russell was a British academic, philosopher, logician, essayist, and social critic. Best-known in the world of philosophy for his groundbreaking work in mathematical logic and analytic philosophy, he also wrote on a variety of other topics from ethics to education. He left his teaching position at Trinity College, Oxford, in 1916 in order to take part in protests against World War I. He was also an outspoken critic of Western involvement in the Vietnam War, and he was the Founding President of the Campaign for Nuclear Disarmament. He was awarded the Nobel Prize for Literature in 1950. With his profound moral and ethical concerns, Russell is the quintessential spiritual Humanist. In what is perhaps his most popular book, *Why I Am Not a Christian* (1927), Russell examines the traditional arguments for the existence of God—finding none of them entirely satisfying—and offers both criticism and appreciation for the person of Jesus as he is portrayed in the Gospels. The book has become a modern classic and a touchstone for all who approach religion skeptically.

Books

Corliss, Lamont. *The Philosophy of Humanism*. Amherst, N.Y.: Humanist Press, 1997.

Knight, Margaret, ed. *Humanist Anthology: From Confucius to Attenborough*. Amherst, N.Y.: Prometheus Books, 1995.

Kopitz, Barbara. *Morning Meditations: Daily Meditations for Spiritual Humanists*. Farmington Hills, Mich.: International Institute for Secular Humanistic Judaism, 1999.

Kurtz, Paul. *The Humanist Manifesto 2000: A Call for a New Planetary Humanism*. Amherst, N.Y.: Prometheus Books, 2000.

Morain, Lloyd. *Humanism: The Next Step*. Amherst, N.Y.: Humanist Press, 1998.

Russell, Bertrand. *Why I Am Not a Christian and Other Essays on Religion and Related Subjects*. New York: Simon & Schuster, 1976.

Periodical

The Humanist
1777 T St., NW
Washington, DC 20009-7125
Telephone: (800) 837-3792
Website: www.thehumanist.org

For More Information

The American Humanist Association
1777 T St., NW
Washington, DC 20009-7125
Telephone: (800) 837-3792
Website: www.americanhumanist.org

› Unitarian Universalist Spirituality

A spirituality with Christian* roots—but without a specifically Christian identity—Unitarian Universalism ("UU") is one of the few places within organized religion where people of a Skeptical-Rational (SR) Spiritual Type might feel quite at home, since this tradition compromises no one's tendency toward skepticism or rationality. In fact, Unitarian Universalists impose no doctrines or creeds upon their members at all. They appeal instead to reason, conscience, and personal experience as ultimate authorities for each individual—rather than any book or governing body.

Unitarian Universalist spiritual practice places great emphasis on social justice and on the importance of diversity—racial, cultural, and otherwise—in our society. Thus UU churches have become welcoming havens for those who desire spiritual community but who cannot in conscience accept the dogmas and creeds imposed by other faiths.

The name *Unitarian Universalist* represents the merging of two compatible denominations—the Unitarians and the Universalists—that took place in 1961. The modern Unitarian movement traces its origins to England and America in the early nineteenth century, in connection with the preaching and writing of the New England minister William Ellery Channing. The term "Unitarian" refers to the belief in the oneness of God (in contrast to the concept of a trinitarian God). The term "Universalist" refers to the idea that salvation is available to everyone, Christian or otherwise.

Unitarian Universalists have not, traditionally, accepted the divinity of Jesus, regarding him as one inspired teacher among many. In many UU churches today, Christian symbols have been removed entirely. Pagan Awareness, Jewish Awareness, and other, similar advocacy groups coexist within the movement to challenge and inspire each other.

We, the member congregations of the Unitarian Universalist Association, covenant to affirm and promote:
The inherent worth and dignity of every person
Justice, equity, and compassion in human relations
Acceptance of one another and encouragement to spiritual growth in our congregations
A free and responsible search for truth and meaning
The right of conscience and the use of the democratic process within our congregations and in society at large
The goal of world community with peace, liberty, and justice for all
Respect for the interdependent web of all existence of which we are a part.

—From the Unitarian Universalist Statement of Principles and Purposes

A Unitarian Universalist You Should Know:
Forrest Church (b.1948)

Forrest Church is senior minister of the Unitarian Universalist Church of All Souls in New York City. The son of the late Senator Frank Church of Idaho—who was one of the early opponents of the Vietnam War—Forrest Church has been a champion of social justice causes. His book *Life Lines: Holding On (and Letting Go)* (Beacon Press) explores the lifelines that can sustain us in times of trouble: deeper connections to neighbors and even strangers, a better understanding of human limits, a larger view of our place in the universe. Church has written or edited more than eighteen other books, including *God and Other Famous Liberals: Recapturing Bible, Flag and Family from the Far Right* (Simon & Schuster).

Books

Buehrens, John A., et al. *A Chosen Faith: An Introduction to Unitarian Universalism.* Boston: Beacon Press: 1998.

Chryssides, George D. *The Elements of Unitarianism.* Boston: Element Books, 1998.

Church, Forrest. *The American Creed: A Spiritual and Patriotic Primer.* New York: St. Martin's, 2002.

———. *Bringing God Home: A Traveler's Guide.* New York: St. Martin's, 2002.

Robinson, David. *The Unitarians and the Univeralists.* Westport, Conn.: Greenwood Press, 1985.

Periodical

World
The Journal of the Unitarian Universalist Association
25 Beacon St.
Boston, MA 02108
Telephone: (617) 948-4611
Website: www.uua.org

For More Information

Unitarian Universalist congregations are found throughout the United States. A congregation near you can also be located by contacting:

The Unitarian Universalist Association
25 Beacon St.
Boston, MA 02108-2800
Telephone: (617) 742-2100
Website: www.uua.org

8 ›

Following Your Own Lead

You are the conductor of your life. You can bring the choir in your being to new levels of brilliance. Align your past beliefs and assumptions with who you really are.

—Karyn D. Kedar[1]

To say that spirituality is practiced means that people engage intentionally in activities that deepen their relationship to the sacred. Often they do so over long periods of time and devote significant amounts of energy to these activities....[I]n many cases, these activities are life-transforming, causing people to engage in service to others and to lead their lives in a worshipful manner.

—Robert Wuthnow[2]

Following your own lead means that you strive to discover the Spiritual Identity that is *already within* you. You don't receive it from somewhere else, you don't need a guru to give it to you, and you will not find it hidden in sacred writings. In short, the answer to the question that we've been concerned with throughout this book— "Who Is My God?"—is as near to you as your own breath, and ultimately just as accessible.

Andrew Harvey, a contemporary scholar of mystical traditions, calls this divine accessibility the "direct path." He writes: "When you discover for yourself how real the direct path is and how it can transform you...your whole life will change and you will discover with wonder and delight why you are here and what you are here for."[3]

Knowing your Spiritual Identity is one thing, but how do we take this knowledge and grow? What will you now do with your Spiritual Identity? How will you make your life more meaningful, and the world a more meaningful place?

This book is based on four premises:

> Each of us is on a spiritual path, whether we know it or not.

> Each of us has a Spiritual Type that shows how we approach our Spiritual Identity.

> Spiritual Identities are dynamic and interactive, usually evolving over time.

> We *follow our own lead* throughout life as we grow, learn, and deepen the meaning of our lives through spiritual practice.

Up to now we have explored the first three of these premises. Now we will look at spiritual practice as the key to growing within your Spiritual Identity.

Getting started in spiritual practice

For starters, it is important not to take your Spiritual Identity and run away with it. When Gandhi said that there are as many spiritual-ities as there are people, he was not suggesting that each of us create a new religion. Neither was he suggesting that we live spiritual lives as islands known only to ourselves. The desire to live a solitary spir-itual life can be strong for people today. This kind of "cocooning" can feel safer than interacting with others. Elizabeth Lesser, cofounder of the Omega Institute, explains it this way:

> Those pursuing a spiritual path are often drawn to solitary wor-
> ship: meditation, retreats, silence. We figure that in solitude we

have to deal only with ourselves, and often that's complex enough. In relationships we have to deal with two complex selves. In groups things can get pretty complex indeed. Yet it is in relationships and groups that we get to demonstrate our real spirituality—love and acceptance of ourselves, love and acceptance of others, and all the rich territory we must cover to learn how to love. There is strength in solitude, and there is sacredness in silence, but we are tested and rewarded most in relationship and communion.[4]

Find the ways that are comfortable for you to test your Spiritual Identity in relationship and communion. Everyone needs help along the way; everyone needs a community in which to grow. This is why religious and spiritual communities exist—there is support there. You should know that it is common to seek spiritual advice in one way or another. Explore the practices that are right for you. Following are some examples found in a variety of religious and spiritual traditions.

Retreat Centers
Retreats are common in many spiritual traditions, and people who stand outside traditions participate in them as well. These are places where people come together to learn from each other for a weekend, a week, or sometimes longer. Single people, couples, and sometimes families are welcome at retreat centers. Often a retreat will center around a topic. For instance, a Christian retreat center might schedule a week centered around contemplative prayer, Celtic Spirituality, or single life. A Jewish retreat center might center a week around kabbalah meditation, Torah study, or dance; a New Consciousness retreat center might have summer courses on yoga, or drumming and painting as spiritual practice. These can be great places to experience a nonthreatening learning environment.

Just Talking

Talking with those closest to you can also be a channel for spiritual growth. To many, this may seem obvious, but for some people there is nothing more difficult than bringing up the subject of spirituality with the ones they love. If you or those around you have difficulty talking about spiritual things, try this: When you are sitting together informally, introduce a topic like "What makes life spiritual?" or, "What makes life worth living?" This is a very nonthreatening, subjective way to start a conversation about Spiritual Identities (in other words, it shouldn't scare off people who avoid the "touchy-feely"), and it can involve everybody in expressing what they think and feel.

Spiritual Direction

If you are already within a religious tradition, you might consider seeking spiritual direction. *Spiritual direction* is the term used to describe a relationship between a seeker and guide, where the guide offers a confidential and secure presence in which spiritual growth can be nurtured. Such guidance is available in a range of religious faiths today. Ask a clergyperson about it.

Many people today are also getting involved in spiritual direction across religious lines. A Christian, for instance, might ask a Buddhist teacher to act as her spiritual director, or vice versa. This kind of relationship can offer many new and enlightening perspectives on your own faith.[5]

New Places for Spiritual Community and Information

The Internet has quickly become a rich source for spirituality. Even large search engines at secular on-line communities, like yahoo.com and msn.com, will periodically host on-line spiritual chats, or interviews with popular spirituality authors, and will help you find spiritual and religious resources on the Web. Other sites are specifically designed to be spiritual resources. Beliefnet.com is one such place to start. There you will find more information about major religious traditions, writings by columnists who represent different spiritual perspectives, conversation on how religion impacts culture, ways to enhance spirituality in family life, even prayer circles—which are posted requests for prayer. The website for *Spirituality & Health* magazine (www.spiritualityhealth.com) is also a terrific source for information, book and movie reviews, e-courses, and discussion groups. But you should be careful not to stop at the Internet. It is better to use it for starting points than as your only spiritual inter-action or community.

Worship—Public and Private

Worship is vital for many people for getting in deeper touch with their Spiritual Identity. The Hindu* term for paying homage to a holy image or person, *darshan*, literally means "to see and be seen by God." This is a good way of thinking about the way to integrate worship into your daily life—by finding those ways in which you can see the Divine all around you, and pay homage in your own, personally meaningful way.

In most religious and spiritual traditions, there are many oppor-tunities for public worship. So many, in many traditions, that you could never be expected to participate in them all. Each worship occa-sion centers around a different theme, or focus, for spiritual life. You may enjoy discovering them. (You may find the following resource useful: *How to Be a Perfect Stranger, 3rd Ed.: The Essential Religious Etiquette Handbook* [SkyLight Paths].)

Study

Most people find benefit in studying scripture, commentaries on scripture, tales of spiritual masters, and the history and customs of traditions as ways of enriching their Spiritual Identities. There are exceptions, however. And if you are one of the two Rational Spiritual Types, you will likely be drawn to study as a spiritual practice, but you might actually benefit more from some of the other, nonintellectual avenues for growth. In either case, there is no end to the wealth of materials available for study within any of the spiritual/religious traditions described in this book.

Engagement with the World

It is important for all people to live their spiritual lives in the midst of others—and to engage with the needs of the world around us. There are always times when being alone is necessary in order to center ourselves, but these solitary times are a preparation for daily life, when we are engaged with people around us. Mindfulness meditation teacher Sylvia Boorstein has said: "Spiritual practice is not about transformation of me, or of anyone else, as individuals—the job is too big and that purpose is too small. I trust that establishing kindness and compassion in any of our individual hearts is on behalf of all beings everywhere. We practice to transform the world."[6]

What is the result? What am I striving for?

The paradoxical thing about the spiritual journey is that these questions may have no easy answer—at least not an answer that can be simply stated. And even if you start out with a clear idea of what you're striving for, that goal can change as you go deeper. Some seek religion out of a need for community and then end up concentrating on inner work. Others start out with an idea of gaining inner peace for themselves, then at some point the focus naturally shifts to helping others.

In this book, we have explored a spectrum of spiritual traditions, each with its own goals firmly in place—whether implicit or plainly expressed. If we were to be so bold as to try to express these goals and condense them into a list, most of us could probably use one or more of the elements of that list (if not all of them) to express what the spiritual search is all about for us:

> I want to become enlightened.

> I want freedom from what enslaves me.

> I want to finally, fully become myself.

> I want to develop my natural capacities.

> I want to help repair the world.

These are goals that can provide enough work for a whole lifetime—and that is an important point to keep in mind. Spiritual insight doesn't always come quickly or easily. You can even expect the goals you begin with to change along the way. But the spiritual path is one where the whole process of getting there is a part of the result. And this is supremely good news for all of us, whether we've been on the journey all of our lives or whether we're just thinking about starting: whatever we call (or don't call) the Divine, no time spent striving toward it is ever wasted. And whether our approach is Faithful, Rational, Skeptical, or Contemplative, the spiritual path is rich with enough adventure and discovery to fill our whole lives.

Notes

Part 1: Finding Your Spiritual Identity

Chapter 1: What Is a Spiritual Identity?

1. H. H. the Dalai Lama, *Ethics for the New Millennium* (New York: Riverhead Books, 1999), 4.

2. Soryu, in a postscript to *The Narrow Road to the Deep North and Other Travel Sketches*, by Basho, trans. by Nobuyuki Yuasa (New York: Penguin Books, 1966), 143.

3. Leo Tolstoy, "My Confession," in *My Confession, My Religion, and The Gospel in Brief* (New York: Thomas Y. Crowell Co., 1899), 57.

4. Kathleen Norris, *Dakota: A Spiritual Geography* (Boston: Houghton Mifflin, 1994), 130–131.

5. Thich Nhat Hanh, *Going Home: Jesus and Buddha as Brothers* (New York: Riverhead Books, 1999), 3–4.

6. Lawrence Kushner, *Honey from the Rock: An Introduction to Jewish Mysticism* (Woodstock, Vt.: Jewish Lights, 2000), 70.

Chapter 2: What Does My Spiritual Identity™ Have to Do with *Religion?*

1. Boorstein quote is taken from *Utne Reader*, July–August 1998, 44.

2. Keating quote is taken from *Utne Reader*, July–August 1998, 44.

3. Marcus J. Borg, *The God We Never Knew: Beyond Dogmatic Religion to a More Authentic Contemporary Faith* (San Francisco: HarperSanFrancisco, 1997), 1–2.

4. Abu Hamid Muhammad Ghazali, quoted in *Pilgrim Souls: A Collection of Spiritual Autobiographies*, ed. by Amy Mandelker and Elizabeth Powers (New York: Simon & Schuster/Touchstone, 1999), 395.

Chapter 3: What Is the Spiritual Identity Self-Test™?

1. Sam Keen, "What You Ask Is Who You Are," *Spirituality & Health*, Spring 2000, 31.

Part 2: Setting Out on Your Path

Introduction

1. Elizabeth Lesser, *The New American Spirituality: A Seeker's Guide* (New York: Random House, 1999), 4.

Chapter 8: Following Your Own Lead

1. Karyn D. Kedar, *God Whispers: Stories of the Soul, Lessons of the Heart* (Woodstock, Vt.: Jewish Lights Publishing, 1999), 91.

2. Robert Wuthnow, *After Heaven: Spirituality in America Since the 1950s* (Berkeley: Univ. of California Press, 1998), 169.

3. Andrew Harvey, *The Direct Path: Creating a Journey to the Divine Through the World's Mystical Traditions* (New York: Broadway Books, 2000), 3.

4. Lesser, *The New American Spirituality*, 390.

5. See Howard A. Addison, *Show Me Your Way: A Complete Guide to Exploring Interfaith Spiritual Direction* (Woodstock, Vt.: SkyLight Paths Publishing, 2000) for more on spiritual direction and interfaith spiritual direction.

6. Quoted in *Forty Days to Begin a Spiritual Life: Today's Most Inspiring Teachers Help You on Your Way* (Woodstock, Vt.: SkyLight Paths Publishing, 2002).

Discussion Guide and Resources to Help You Along the Way

Discussion Guide

What Influences Helped to Shape Your Spiritual Identity?

Reflecting on your experiences in childhood and young adulthood may give you a clue about the Spiritual Identity that you choose to embrace. Whether you decide to follow a different spiritual path or you continue (or return to) the spiritual tradition of your earlier years, asking yourself the following questions can assist you in understanding your own spiritual development.

> Was a particular day of the week set aside for religious services? Was that day a "family day" spent together? How did you feel about that?

> As you grew older, how often did you participate in religious services? Was it a struggle or a pleasure to set that time aside?

> What rules of your faith tradition did you have to follow that you liked or did not like?

> Did your family say grace, blessings, or other prayers at mealtimes? How did you feel about participating?

> Did your family or your religious education teachers encourage independent reading and study of your faith tradition?

> Was there an adult outside your family who served as a spiritual mentor for you? A godparent, sponsor, teacher, youth leader, or clergyperson?

> Were you a member of a faith-affiliated youth group or community-service group? Was this a meaningful experience for you?

> If you have chosen to follow a different spiritual path from that of your earlier years, how has that decision affected your relationships with your family and friends?

> What other aspects of growing up in your particular spiritual tradition do you particularly remember? What do you miss? What were you happy to leave behind?

> How have you incorporated valued traditions from your younger life into your present spiritual practice?

Establishing Your Spiritual Goals

Your Spiritual Goals

Focus on your spiritual goals by completing this simple worksheet. You may want to keep a spiritual diary to record your efforts at growing consciously in body, mind, and spirit.

My goals to achieve a spiritually satisfying life are:

Consciousness of the body

› What activities will help me feel more spiritually connected? (For example, walking a labyrinth, ritual bowing, chanting, using prayer beads)

Consciousness of the mind

› What exercises will help my mind to focus on spirituality and inner peace? (For example, meditation, daily readings, journaling, mindful walking and eating)

Consciousness of the soul

> ❯ What practices will help me to access the Divine on my
> path to spiritual growth? (For example, personal prayer at
> specific times each day, attending group prayer services,
> finding a spiritual director)

Books of Special Interest to Spiritual Seekers

Addison, Howard A. *Show Me Your Way: The Complete Guide to Exploring Interfaith Spiritual Direction.* Woodstock, Vt.: SkyLight Paths, 2000.

Boorstein, Sylvia. *Pay Attention, for Goodness' Sake: Practicing the Perfections of the Heart—The Buddhist Path of Kindness.* New York: Ballantine Books, 2002.

Brussat, Frederic, and Mary Ann Brussat. *Spiritual Literacy: Reading the Sacred in Everyday Life.* New York: Scribner, 1996.

———. *Spiritual Rx: Prescriptions for Living a Meaningful Life.* New York: Hyperion Press, 2000.

Cooper, David A. *A Heart of Stillness: A Complete Guide to Learning the Art of Meditation.* Woodstock, Vt.: SkyLight Paths, 1999.

Cooper, Howard. *The Alphabet of Paradise: An A-Z of Spirituality for Everyday Life.* Woodstock, Vt.: SkyLight Paths, 2003.

Foster, Richard J. *Streams of Living Water: Celebrating the Great Traditions of Christian Faith.* San Francisco: HarperSanFrancisco, 1998.

Guerrero, Diana L. *What Animals Can Teach Us about Spirituality: Inspiring Lessons from Wild and Tame Creatures.* Woodstock, Vt.: SkyLight Paths, 2003.

Harnden, Philip. *Journeys of Simplicity: Traveling Light with Thomas Merton, Basho, Edward Abbey, Annie Dillard and Others.* Woodstock, Vt.: SkyLight Paths, 2003.

Harvey, Andrew. *A Walk with Four Spiritual Guides: Krishna, Buddha, Jesus, and Ramakrishna.* Woodstock, Vt.: SkyLight Paths, 2003.

Johnson, Cait. *Earth, Water, Fire, and Air: Essential Ways of Connecting to Spirit.* Woodstock, Vt.: SkyLight Paths, 2003.

Lesser, Elizabeth. *The New American Spirituality: A Seeker's Guide.* New York: Random House, 1999.

Lindahl, Kay. *The Sacred Art of Listening: Forty Reflections for Cultivating a Spiritual Practice.* Woodstock, Vt.: SkyLight Paths, 2002.

Matlins, Stuart M., ed. *The Jewish Lights Spirituality Handbook: A Guide to Understanding, Exploring and Living a Spiritual Life.* Woodstock, Vt.: Jewish Lights Publishing, 2001.

Norris, Kathleen. *Amazing Grace: A Vocabulary of Faith.* New York: Riverhead Books, 1998.

Rifkin, Ira, ed. *Spiritual Innovators: Seventy-Five Extraordinary People Who Changed the World in the Past Century.* Woodstock, Vt.: SkyLight Paths, 2002.

Shaw, Maura D., ed. *Forty Days to Begin a Spiritual Life: Today's Most Inspiring Teachers Help You on Your Way.* Woodstock, Vt.: SkyLight Paths, 2002.

Strand, Clark. *Meditation without Gurus: A Guide to the Heart of Practice.* Woodstock, Vt.: SkyLight Paths, 2003.

Sweeney, Jon M. *Praying with Our Hands: Twenty-One Practices of Embodied Prayer from the World's Spiritual Traditions.* Woodstock, Vt.: SkyLight Paths, 2000.

Wakefield, Dan. *Spiritually Incorrect: Finding God in All the Wrong Places.* Woodstock, Vt.: SkyLight Paths, 2003.

Index

Using the Spiritual Identity Self-Test™ in Your Group or Organization

If you are interested in becoming a Spiritual Identity Self-Test™ Facilitator, please contact:

SkyLight Paths Publishing
P.O. Box 237
Woodstock, VT 05091
Fax: (802) 457-4004
Tel: (802) 457-4000
www.skylightpaths.com

Share with Us Your Experience of Taking the Spiritual Identity Self-Test™ by writing:

The Editors
SkyLight Paths Publishing
P.O. Box 237
Woodstock, VT 05091
Fax: (802) 457-4004
Tel: (802) 457-4000
www.skylightpaths.com

About SKYLIGHT PATHS Publishing

SkyLight Paths Publishing is creating a place where people of different spiritual traditions come together for challenge and inspiration, a place where we can help each other understand the mystery that lies at the heart of our existence.

Through spirituality, our religious beliefs are increasingly becoming a part of our lives—rather than *apart* from our lives. While many of us may be more interested than ever in spiritual growth, we may be less firmly planted in traditional religion. Yet, we do want to deepen our relationship to the sacred, to learn from our own as well as from other faith traditions, and to practice in new ways.

SkyLight Paths sees both believers and seekers as a community that increasingly transcends traditional boundaries of religion and denomination—people wanting to learn from each other, *walking together, finding the way.*

We at SkyLight Paths take great care to produce beautiful books that present meaningful spiritual content in a form that reflects the art of making high quality books. Therefore, we want to acknowledge those who contributed to the production of this book.

PRODUCTION
Tim Holtz & Bridgett Taylor

EDITORIAL
Sarah McBride, Maura D. Shaw & Emily Wichland

COVER DESIGN
Brownwen Battaglia, Scituate, Massachusetts

TEXT DESIGN
Chelsea Cloeter, Scotia, New York

PRINTING & BINDING
Versa Press, East Peoria, Illinois

Other Interesting Books—Spirituality

Lighting the Lamp of Wisdom: *A Week Inside a Yoga Ashram*
by *John Ittner*; Foreword by *Dr. David Frawley*

This insider's guide to Hindu spiritual life takes you into a typical week of retreat inside a yoga ashram to demystify the experience and show you what to expect from your own visit. Includes a discussion of worship services, meditation and yoga classes, chanting and music, work practice, and more.

6 x 9, 192 pp, b/w photographs, Quality PB, ISBN 1-893361-52-7 **$15.95**;
HC, ISBN 1-893361-37-3 **$24.95**

Waking Up: *A Week Inside a Zen Monastery*
by *Jack Maguire*; Foreword by *John Daido Loori, Roshi*

An essential guide to what it's like to spend a week inside a Zen Buddhist monastery.
6 x 9, 224 pp, b/w photographs, Quality PB, ISBN 1-893361-55-1 **$16.95**;
HC, ISBN 1-893361-13-6 **$21.95**

Making a Heart for God: *A Week Inside a Catholic Monastery*
by *Dianne Aprile*; Foreword by *Brother Patrick Hart, OCSO*

This essential guide to experiencing life in a Catholic monastery takes you to the Abbey of Gethsemani—the Trappist monastery in Kentucky that was home to author Thomas Merton—to explore the details. "More balanced and informative than the popular *The Cloister Walk* by Kathleen Norris." —*Choice: Current Reviews for Academic Libraries*

6 x 9, 224 pp, b/w photographs, Quality PB, ISBN 1-893361-49-7 **$16.95**;
HC, ISBN 1-893361-14-4 **$21.95**

Come and Sit: *A Week Inside Meditation Centers*
by *Marcia Z. Nelson*; Foreword by *Wayne Teasdale*

The insider's guide to meditation in a variety of different spiritual traditions. Traveling through Buddhist, Hindu, Christian, Jewish, and Sufi traditions, this essential guide takes you to different meditation centers to meet the teachers and students and learn about the practices, demystifying the meditation experience.

6 x 9, 224 pp, b/w photographs, Quality PB, ISBN 1-893361-35-7 **$16.95**

Or phone, fax, mail or e-mail to: SKYLIGHT PATHS Publishing
Sunset Farm Offices, Route 4 • P.O. Box 237 • Woodstock, Vermont 05091
Tel: (802) 457-4000 • Fax: (802) 457-4004 • www.skylightpaths.com
Credit card orders: (800) 962-4544 (8:30AM–5:30PM ET Monday–Friday)
Generous discounts on quantity orders. SATISFACTION GUARANTEED. Prices subject to change.

Religious Etiquette/Reference

How to Be a Perfect Stranger, 3rd Edition
The Essential Religious Etiquette Handbook
Edited by *Stuart M. Matlins* and *Arthur J. Magida*

The indispensable guidebook to help the well-meaning guest when visiting other people's religious ceremonies.

A straightforward guide to the rituals and celebrations of the major religions and denominations in the United States and Canada from the perspective of an interested guest of any other faith, based on information obtained from authorities of each religion. Belongs in every living room, library, and office.

COVERS:

African American Methodist Churches • Assemblies of God • Baha'i • Baptist • Buddhist • Christian Church (Disciples of Christ) • Christian Science (Church of Christ, Scientist) • Churches of Christ • Episcopalian and Anglican • Hindu • Islam • Jehovah's Witnesses • Jewish • Lutheran • Mennonite/Amish • Methodist • Mormon (Church of Jesus Christ of Latter-day Saints) • Native American/First Nations • Orthodox Churches • Pentecostal Church of God • Presbyterian • Quaker (Religious Society of Friends) • Reformed Church in America/Canada • Roman Catholic • Seventh-day Adventist • Sikh • Unitarian Universalist • United Church of Canada • United Church of Christ

6 x 9, 432 pp, Quality PB, ISBN 1-893361-67-5 **$19.95**

Also available:

The Perfect Stranger's Guide to Funerals and Grieving Practices
A Guide to Etiquette in Other People's Religious Ceremonies
Edited by *Stuart M. Matlins*
6 x 9, 240 pp, Quality PB, ISBN 1-893361-20-9 **$16.95**

The Perfect Stranger's Guide to Wedding Ceremonies
A Guide to Etiquette in Other People's Religious Ceremonies
Edited by *Stuart M. Matlins*
6 x 9, 208 pp, Quality PB, ISBN 1-893361-19-5 **$16.95**

Spiritual Biography

The Life of Evelyn Underhill
An Intimate Portrait of the Groundbreaking Author of Mysticism
by *Margaret Cropper;* Foreword by *Dana Greene*

Evelyn Underhill was a passionate writer and teacher who wrote elegantly on mysticism, worship, and devotional life. This is the story of how she made her way toward spiritual maturity, from her early days of agnosticism to the years when her influence was felt throughout the world. 6 x 9, 288 pp, 5 b/w photos, Quality PB, ISBN 1-893361-70-5 **$18.95**

Zen Effects: *The Life of Alan Watts*
by *Monica Furlong*

The first and only full-length biography of one of the most charismatic spiritual leaders of the twentieth century—now back in print!

Through his widely popular books and lectures, Alan Watts (1915–1973) did more to introduce Eastern philosophy and religion to Western minds than any figure before or since. Here is the only biography of this charismatic figure, who served as Zen teacher, Anglican priest, lecturer, academic, entertainer, a leader of the San Francisco renaissance, and author of more than 30 books, including *The Way of Zen, Psychotherapy East and West* and *The Spirit of Zen.* 6 x 9, 264 pp, Quality PB, ISBN 1-893361-32-2 **$16.95**

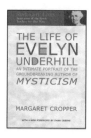  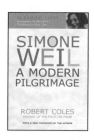 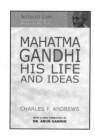

Simone Weil: *A Modern Pilgrimage*
by *Robert Coles*

The extraordinary life of the spiritual philosopher who's been called both saint and madwoman.

The French writer and philosopher Simone Weil (1906–1943) devoted her life to a search for God—while avoiding membership in organized religion. Robert Coles' intriguing study of Weil details her short, eventful life, and is an insightful portrait of the beloved and controversial thinker whose life and writings influenced many (from T. S. Eliot to Adrienne Rich to Albert Camus), and continue to inspire seekers everywhere. 6 x 9, 208 pp, Quality PB, ISBN 1-893361-34-9 **$16.95**

Mahatma Gandhi: *His Life and Ideas*
by *Charles F. Andrews;* Foreword by *Dr. Arun Gandhi*

An intimate biography of one of the greatest social and religious reformers of the modern world.

Examines from a contemporary Christian activist's point of view the religious ideas and political dynamics that influenced the birth of the peaceful resistance movement, the primary tool that Gandhi and the people of his homeland would use to gain India its freedom from British rule. An ideal introduction to the life and life's work of this great spiritual leader. 6 x 9, 336 pp, 5 b/w photos, Quality PB, ISBN 1-893361-89-6 **$18.95**

Spiritual Practice

The Sacred Art of Bowing
Preparing to Practice
by *Andi Young*

This informative and inspiring introduction to bowing—and related spiritual practices—shows you how to do it, why it's done, and what spiritual benefits it has to offer. Incorporates interviews, personal stories, illustrations of bowing in practice, advice on how you can incorporate bowing into your daily life, and how bowing can deepen spiritual understanding.
5½ x 8½, 128 pp, b/w illus., Quality PB, ISBN 1-893361-82-9 **$14.95**

Praying with Our Hands: *Twenty-One Practices of Embodied Prayer from the World's Spiritual Traditions*
by *Jon M. Sweeney*; Photographs by *Jennifer J. Wilson*;
Foreword by *Mother Tessa Bielecki*; Afterword by *Taitetsu Unno, Ph.D.*

A spiritual guidebook for bringing prayer into our bodies.

This inspiring book of reflections and accompanying photographs shows us twenty-one simple ways of using our hands to speak to God, to enrich our devotion and ritual. All express the various approaches of the world's religious traditions to bringing the body into worship. Spiritual traditions represented include Anglican, Sufi, Zen, Roman Catholic, Yoga, Shaker, Hindu, Jewish, Pentecostal, Eastern Orthodox, and many others.
8 x 8, 96 pp, 22 duotone photographs, Quality PB, ISBN 1-893361-16-0 **$16.95**

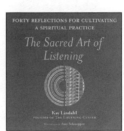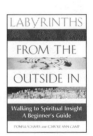

The Sacred Art of Listening
Forty Reflections for Cultivating a Spiritual Practice
by *Kay Lindahl*; Illustrations by *Amy Schnapper*

More than ever before, we need to embrace the skills and practice of listening. You will learn to: Speak clearly from your heart • Communicate with courage and compassion • Heighten your awareness for deep listening • Enhance your ability to listen to people with different belief systems. 8 x 8, 160 pp, Illus., Quality PB, ISBN 1-893361-44-6 **$16.99**

Labyrinths from the Outside In
Walking to Spiritual Insight—a Beginner's Guide
by *Donna Schaper* and *Carole Ann Camp*

The user-friendly, interfaith guide to making and using labyrinths— for meditation, prayer, and celebration.

Labyrinth walking is a spiritual exercise *anyone* can do. This accessible guide unlocks the mysteries of the labyrinth for all of us, providing ideas for using the labyrinth walk for prayer, meditation, and celebrations to mark the most important moments in life. Includes instructions for making a labyrinth of your own and finding one in your area.
6 x 9, 208 pp, b/w illus. and photographs, Quality PB, ISBN 1-893361-18-7 **$16.95**

SkyLight Illuminations Series
Andrew Harvey, series editor

Offers today's spiritual seeker an enjoyable entry into the great classic texts of the world's spiritual traditions. Each classic is presented in an accessible translation, with facing pages of guided commentary from experts, giving you the keys you need to understand the history, context, and meaning of the text. This series enables readers of all backgrounds to experience and understand classic spiritual texts directly, and to make them a part of their lives. Andrew Harvey writes the foreword to each volume, an insightful, personal introduction to each classic.

Bhagavad Gita: *Annotated & Explained*
Translation by *Shri Purohit Swami;* Annotation by *Kendra Crossen Burroughs*

"The very best Gita for first-time readers." —Ken Wilber

Millions of people turn daily to India's most beloved holy book, whose universal appeal has made it popular with non-Hindus and Hindus alike. This edition introduces you to the characters; explains references and philosophical terms; shares the interpretations of famous spiritual leaders and scholars; and more. 5½ x 8½, 192 pp, Quality PB, ISBN 1-893361-28-4 **$16.95**

  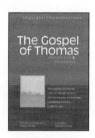 

The Way of a Pilgrim: *Annotated & Explained*
Translation and annotation by *Gleb Pokrovsky*

This classic of Russian spirituality is the delightful account of one man who sets out to learn the prayer of the heart—also known as the "Jesus prayer"—and how the practice transforms his life. 5½ x 8½, 160 pp, Quality PB, ISBN 1-893361-31-4 **$14.95**

The Gospel of Thomas: *Annotated & Explained*
Translation and annotation by *Stevan Davies*

Discovered in 1945, this collection of aphoristic sayings sheds new light on the origins of Christianity and the intriguing figure of Jesus, portraying the Kingdom of God as a present fact about the world, rather than a future promise or future threat. This edition guides you through the text with annotations that focus on the meaning of the sayings. 5½ x 8½, 192 pp, Quality PB, ISBN 1-893361-45-4 **$16.95**

Rumi and Islam: *Selections from His Stories, Poems, and Discourses— Annotated & Explained*
Translation and annotation by *Ibrahim Gamard*

Offers a new way of thinking about Rumi's poetry. Ibrahim Gamard focuses on Rumi's place within the Sufi tradition of Islam, providing you with insight into the mystical side of the religion—one that has love of God at its core and sublime wisdom teachings as its pathways. 5½ x 8½, 240 pp, Quality PB, ISBN 1-59473-002-4 **$15.99**

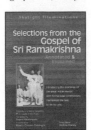

Meditation/Prayer

Finding Grace at the Center: *The Beginning of Centering Prayer*

by *M. Basil Pennington*, OCSO, *Thomas Keating*, OCSO, and *Thomas E. Clarke*, SJ

The book that helped launch the Centering Prayer "movement." Explains the prayer of *The Cloud of Unknowing*, posture and relaxation, the three simple rules of centering prayer, and how to cultivate centering prayer throughout all aspects of your life.

5 x 7¼,112 pp, HC, ISBN 1-893361-69-1 **$14.95**

Prayers to an Evolutionary God

by *William Cleary*; Afterword by *Diarmuid O'Murchu*

How is it possible to pray when God is dislocated from heaven, dispersed all around us, and more of a creative force than an all-knowing father? In this unique collection of eighty prose prayers and related commentary, William Cleary considers new ways of thinking about God and the world around us. Inspired by the spiritual and scientific teachings of Diarmuid O'Murchu and Tielhard de Chardin, Cleary reveals that religion and science can be combined to create an expanding view of the universe—an evolutionary faith.

6 x 9, 188 pp, Hardcover, ISBN 1-59473-006-7 **$19.99**

  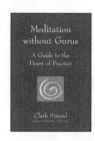 

Meditation without Gurus
A Guide to the Heart of Practice

by *Clark Strand*

Short, compelling reflections show you how to make meditation a part of your daily life, without the complication of gurus, mantras, retreats, or treks to distant mountains. This enlightening book strips the practice down to its essential heart—simplicity, lightness, and peace—showing you that the most important part of practice is not whether you can get in the full lotus position, but rather your ability to become fully present in the moment.

5½ x 8½, 192 pp, Quality PB, ISBN 1-893361-93-4 **$16.95**

Prayer for People Who Think Too Much
A Guide to Everyday, Anywhere Prayer from the World's Faith Traditions

by *Mitch Finley*

Helps us make prayer a natural part of daily living.

Takes a thoughtful look at how each major faith tradition incorporates prayer into *daily* life. Explores Christian sacraments, Jewish holy days, Muslim daily prayer, "mindfulness" in Buddhism, and more, to help you better understand and enhance your own prayer practices. "I love this book." —Caroline M. Myss, Ph.D., author of *Anatomy of the Spirit*

5½ x 8½, 224 pp, Quality PB, ISBN 1-893361-21-7 **$16.95**; HC, ISBN 1-893361-00-4 **$21.95**

Children's Spirituality

Becoming Me: *A Story of Creation*

by *Martin Boroson*
Full-color illus. by *Christopher Gilvan-Cartwright*

For ages 4 & up

Told in the personal "voice" of the Creator, here is a story about creation and relationship that is about each one of us. In simple words and with radiant illustrations, the Creator tells an intimate story about love, about friendship and playing, about our world—and about ourselves. And with each turn of the page, we're reminded that we just might be closer to our Creator than we think!

8 x 10, 32 pp, Full-color illus., HC, ISBN 1-893361-11-X **$16.95**

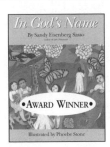

Noah's Wife
The Story of Naamah
by *Sandy Eisenberg Sasso*
Full-color illus. by *Bethanne Andersen*

For ages 4 & up

This new story, based on an ancient text, opens readers' religious imaginations to new ideas about the well-known story of the Flood. When God tells Noah to bring the animals of the world onto the ark, God also calls on Naamah, Noah's wife, to save each plant on Earth. "A lovely tale.... Children of all ages should be drawn to this parable for our times."
—Tomie de Paola, artist/author of books for children
9 x 12, 32 pp, HC, Full-color illus., ISBN 1-58023-134-9 **$16.95**

In God's Name
by *Sandy Eisenberg Sasso*; Full-color illus. by *Phoebe Stone*

For ages 4 & up

Like an ancient myth in its poetic text and vibrant illustrations, this award-winning modern fable about the search for God's name celebrates the diversity and, at the same time, the unity of all the people of the world.
9 x 12, 32 pp, HC, Full-color illus., ISBN 1-879045-26-5 **$16.95**

Also available in Spanish:
El nombre de Dios 9 x 12, 32 pp, HC, Full-color illus., ISBN 1-893361-63-2 **$16.95**

The 11th Commandment
Wisdom from Our Children
by *The Children of America*

For ages 4 & up

"If there were an Eleventh Commandment, what would it be?" Children of many religious denominations across America answer this question—in their own drawings and words. "A rare book of spiritual celebration for all people, of all ages, for all time." —*Bookviews*
8 x 10, 48 pp, HC, Full-color illus., ISBN 1-879045-46-X **$16.95**

Children's Spirituality

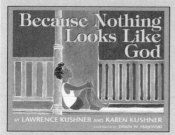

Because Nothing Looks Like God

by *Lawrence and Karen Kushner*
Full-color illus. by
Dawn W. Majewski

For ages 4 & up

MULTICULTURAL, NONDENOMINATIONAL, NONSECTARIAN

Real-life examples of happiness and sadness—from goodnight stories, to the hope and fear felt the first time at bat, to the closing moments of life—introduce children to the possibilities of spiritual life. A vibrant way for children—and their adults—to explore what, where, and how God is in our lives.

11 x 8½, 32 pp, HC, Full-color illus., ISBN 1-58023-092-X **$16.95**

*Also available: **Teacher's Guide,** 8½ x 11, 22 pp, PB, ISBN 1-58023-140-3 **$6.95** For ages 5–8*

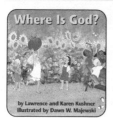   

Where Is God? (A Board Book)

For ages 0–4

by *Lawrence and Karen Kushner*; Full-color illus. by *Dawn W. Majewski*

A gentle way for young children to explore how God is with us every day, in every way. Abridged from *Because Nothing Looks Like God* by Lawrence and Karen Kushner and specially adapted to board book format to delight and inspire young readers.

5 x 5, 24 pp, Board, Full-color illus., ISBN 1-893361-17-9 **$7.95**

What Does God Look Like? (A Board Book)

For ages 0–4

by *Lawrence and Karen Kushner*; Full-color illus. by *Dawn W. Majewski*

A simple way for young children to explore the ways that we "see" God. Abridged from *Because Nothing Looks Like God* by Lawrence and Karen Kushner and specially adapted to board book format to delight and inspire young readers.

5 x 5, 24 pp, Board, Full-color illus., ISBN 1-893361-23-3 **$7.95**

How Does God Make Things Happen? (A Board Book)

For ages 0–4

by *Lawrence and Karen Kushner*; Full-color illus. by *Dawn W. Majewski*

A charming invitation for young children to explore how God makes things happen in our world. Abridged from *Because Nothing Looks Like God* by Lawrence and Karen Kushner and specially adapted to board book format to delight and inspire young readers.

5 x 5, 24 pp, Board, Full-color illus., ISBN 1-893361-24-1 **$7.95**

What Is God's Name? (A Board Book)

For ages 0–4

by *Sandy Eisenberg Sasso*; Full-color illus. by *Phoebe Stone*

Everyone and everything in the world has a name. What is God's name? Abridged from the award-winning *In God's Name* by Sandy Eisenberg Sasso and specially adapted to board book format to delight and inspire young readers.

5 x 5, 24 pp, Board, Full-color illus., ISBN 1-893361-10-1 **$7.95**

Children's Spiritual Biography

Ten Amazing People
And How They Changed the World

For ages 7 & up

by *Maura D. Shaw*; Foreword by *Dr. Robert Coles*
Full-color illus. by *Stephen Marchesi*

Black Elk • Dorothy Day • Malcolm X • Mahatma Gandhi •
Martin Luther King, Jr. • Mother Teresa • Janusz Korczak •
Desmond Tutu • Thich Nhat Hanh • Albert Schweitzer

This vivid, inspirational, and authoritative book will open new possibilities for children by telling the stories of how ten of the past century's greatest leaders changed the world in important ways.

8½, x 11, 48 pp, HC, Full-color illus., ISBN 1-893361-47-0 **$17.95**

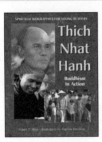

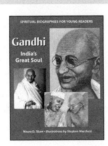

• AWARD WINNER •

A new series: Spiritual Biographies for Young Readers

Thich Nhat Hanh
Buddhism in Action

For ages 7 & up

by *Maura D. Shaw*; Full-color illus. by *Stephen Marchesi*

Warm illustrations, photos, age-appropriate activities, and Thich Nhat Hanh's own poems introduce a great man to children in a way they can understand and enjoy. Includes a list of important words to know and a timeline of important events in the life of Thich Nhat Hanh.
6¾ x 8¾, 32 pp, HC, Full-color illus., ISBN 1-893361-87-X **$12.95**

Gandhi
India's Great Soul

For ages 7 & up

by *Maura D. Shaw*; Full-color illus. by *Stephen Marchesi*

There are a number of biographies of Gandhi written for young readers, but this is the only one that balances a simple text with illustrations, photographs, and activities that encourage children and adults to talk about how to make changes happen without violence. Introduces children to important concepts of freedom, equality, and justice among people of all backgrounds and religions.
6¾ x 8 ¾, 32 pp, HC, Full-color illus., ISBN 1-893361-91-8 **$12.95**

For younger children:

Where Does God Live?

For ages 3–6

by *August Gold* and *Matthew J. Perlman*

Using simple, everyday examples that children can relate to, this colorful book helps young readers develop a personal understanding of God.
10 x 8½, 32 pp, Quality PB, Full-color photo illus., ISBN 1-893361-39-X **$8.95**

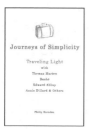

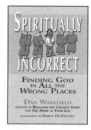